FLAVOR FIRST

FLAVORFIRST

CUT CALORIES AND BOOST FLAVOR WITH
75 DELICIOUS, ALL-NATURAL RECIPES

CHERYL FORBERG, RD

RODALE.

Rodale books may be purchased for business or promotional use or for special sales. For information, please write to: Special Markets Department, Rodale Inc., 733 Third Avenue, New York, NY 10017.

Printed in the United States of America

Rodale Inc. makes every effort to use acid-free ♾, recycled paper ♻.

Book design by Christina Gaugler

Photographs by Rita Maas

Food styling by Vivian Lui and prop styling by Pam Morris

Library of Congress Cataloging-in-Publication Data

Forberg, Cheryl.

    Flavor first : cut calories and boost flavor with 75 delicious, all-natural recipes / Cheryl Forberg.

        p.   cm.

    Includes bibliographical references and index.

    ISBN-13 978–1–60529–149–9 pbk

    ISBN-10 1–60529–149–8 pbk

    1. Cooking (Natural foods)   2. Low-calorie diet—Recipes.   3. Health.   I. Title.

TX741.F665   2011

641.5'636—dc22   2011001098

Distributed to the trade by Macmillan

2 4 6 8 10 9 7 5 3 1   paperback

We inspire and enable people to improve their lives and the world around them.

www.rodalebooks.com

To Paul

CONTENTS

FOREWORD

I've had the pleasure of eating dinner at my friend Cheryl Forberg's house several times. I call it an adventure in "healthy indulgence," because even though her food tastes rich and satisfying, it's as wholesome as it is delicious. Spending time in her kitchen reminds me that creating delicious flavors doesn't have to rely on expensive ingredients or intensive preparation methods. Sometimes, the simplest flavors are the best ones.

The magical thing about cooking is that anyone can become a celebrated chef in his or her own kitchen with just a handful of simple tricks. Culinary success is built on a few fundamentals—planning ahead; using fresh, high-quality ingredients; and tasting everything as you go along. In *Flavor First,* Cheryl Forberg offers her readers more than just a book of healthy recipes; she teaches us how to create wholesome, satisfying, flavorful food.

When I was a student at the Culinary Institute of America, one of my instructors used to chide me for adding too much of one ingredient or not enough of another to my assigned recipes. One day he sneered in exasperation, "Hunter, you're a cook, not a mechanic. Taste as you go; don't simply follow the recipe." Maybe it was his tough love, or maybe his comments were the wake-up call I needed to relax and enjoy myself in the kitchen—but either way, I began to taste *everything* I cooked, a habit I still practice today. Whether it's the oatmeal I make for my kids in the morning or a complex sauce I'm creating for one of my restaurants—I am always tasting and adjusting as I go.

After culinary school, I had the pleasure of working for Barbara Tropp at San Francisco's China Moon Cafe. Barbara, often called the Julia Child of Chinese cuisine, had a magnificent palate. She understood flavor from both an intellectual and a sensory perspective. Chef Barbara taught me the art of creating subtle, complex flavors, and, perhaps most important, she taught me to slow down and savor my meals. Eating slowly is a healthier way to eat, and savoring food is the best way to understand the flavors you like and how to replicate them.

Today I own a culinary development company called Culinary Craft. I develop restaurant and retail food concepts for food celebrities like Wolfgang Puck and Martha Stewart. In my position, I've witnessed many culinary trends come and go, but the one thing that never goes out of style is flavor. I often say to friends and clients that flavor is free. It's free because the *pantry of flavor*—which includes fresh herbs and spices, citrus juice and zest, vinegars and sauces—is relatively low in calories, sodium, and fat. In fact, with very little financial and caloric investment, you can turn an uninspired grilled halibut fillet into a restaurant-worthy dish. Chop some fresh basil or flat parsley leaves, mince a clove of garlic, and add a pinch of lemon zest. The Italians call this *gremolata . . .* and it's pure, fresh flavor.

Another chef's secret is that more color equals more flavor. By caramelizing the natural sugars in meats and vegetables on the grill or in a hot oven, you coax out more intense, concentrated flavors. Try tasting a raw white mushroom compared with a roasted mushroom. Even without added salt or oil, the difference is noticeable. If you toss those mushrooms together with some garlic, ginger, and a bit of peanut oil before roasting, the flavor difference becomes revolutionary. You can achieve similar results by roasting cherry tomatoes, bell peppers, carrots, brussels sprouts, broccoli, or almost any other vegetable. In fact, the simple, delicious pleasure of a perfectly roasted vegetable may inspire you to try vegetables and recipes you've never eaten before.

Consider this book the key that unlocks your taste buds and gives you all the tools and techniques you need to create a new world of flavor. With it, you'll make the same transformation I did—you'll graduate beyond the mechanics of recipe execution to become a true cook.

Chef Andrew Hunter
President, Culinary Craft
Partner, Flavor First Food Company

INTRODUCTION

After 11 seasons as the nutritionist for NBC's *The Biggest Loser,* I've learned a great deal about the typical eating habits of many Americans, particularly the habits that cause weight gain. When I sit down with the contestants at the Biggest Loser Ranch for their one-on-one personal nutrition consultations, we review their food journals, and I help them understand how their food choices—both good and bad—impact their waistlines and their overall health.

Oftentimes, they're shocked to discover just how many calories they've been taking in, as well as the unlikely sources of those extra calories. Some contestants are stunned to learn that they've been consuming an entire day's worth of calories in their beverages alone, while others discover that the seemingly "healthy choices" they've been making aren't nearly as nutritious or as low in calories as they'd assumed.

A surprising number of these excess calories come in the form of sauces, dressings, oils, marinades, and condiments—which, if not used carefully, can turn a healthy meal into a nutritional nightmare and, over time, add up to pounds of extra weight. For example, consider the bowl of French onion dip that we enjoy with our crudités, the dab of creamy mayo we use to enliven our sandwich, or even the bottled Caesar vinaigrette that seems "healthier" than creamy ranch. Just ¼ cup of the dip can have as many as 200 calories (most of which come from fat), while a mere tablespoon of mayo can add 90 calories (*all* of them fat) to your otherwise virtuous

turkey sandwich. Even that Caesar vinaigrette can contain 150 calories in a modest 2-tablespoon serving. And when you don't keep careful track of portion sizes, the calories add up even faster.

One reason why we always seem to be pouring, slathering, and dipping our foods with tasty extras is because our taste buds have become accustomed to the intense flavors of highly processed foods—from salty to sweet, spicy to creamy. Most dips and condiments available at the grocery store are loaded with sodium, fat, and refined sugars. And the more fake food we eat, the more our taste buds crave outrageous, manufactured flavors that can overwhelm the more subtle, natural flavors of fresh fruits and vegetables, whole grains, and healthy proteins.

Many of my clients are reluctant to part with their highly processed favorites because they don't think their cravings can be satisfied with "healthy food." But it's a misconception that simple, nutritious foods can't be absolutely bursting with flavor. And that's why I wanted to write this book.

In *Flavor First,* you'll learn how to tease out and enhance the natural, delicious flavors of fresh foods and create plenty of zing—naturally. From creating your own spice rubs and marinades, to whipping up delicious sauces and vinaigrettes, to learning simple cooking techniques that will add layers of flavor to your food, *Flavor First* will give you plenty of options for adding some zest to your weeknight routine and show you that healthy food is anything but bland.

Now, let's get cooking!

THE ESSENTIALS OF HEALTHY FLAVOR

Cooking fast, flavorful, healthy food is easier than you think. You don't need to invest a fortune in kitchen accessories or spend hours scouring obscure stores for fancy ingredients in order to create dishes that are scrumptious *and* wholesome.

Rather, armed with a few basic principles and equipped with a set of essential kitchen tools, you'll be ready not only to make the flavorful recipes in this book, but also to create and expand your own repertoire of healthy, crowd-pleasing dishes.

In this chapter, you'll learn everything you need to create flavor and cook with confidence.

- We'll look at how tastes and textures interplay to create a satisfying flavor.

- We'll take a virtual trip around the world to discover exotic flavor profiles.

- We'll explore a variety of cooking methods and their impact on flavor and nutrition.

- We'll discuss which kitchen tools are essential— and which aren't.

- And finally, we'll tour the *Flavor First* pantry for an overview of the staples you should always have on hand to whip up zesty, healthy dishes any night of the week.

WHAT IS FLAVOR?

When we describe food as flavorful, we mean that it's appetizing to eat—it appeals to our senses, and once we've tasted it, we want to keep eating. But where does flavor come from and how do we experience it?

The attractive quality we call flavor is actually a combination of senses—not only what our taste buds taste, but what we smell and the tactile sensations we feel as we eat. After all, our noses and mouths share an airway that allows both smells and tastes to commingle as we eat, giving us the ability to register a wide range of flavors based on different combinations of scents and tastes. Even our sense of touch plays a role in the way we enjoy foods—as anyone who's ever had a craving for crunchy chips, a pillowy soft slice of bread, or a cool, creamy bowl of ice cream can attest!

Let's take a closer look at how our senses impact our perception of flavor.

Taste

Although we can potentially identify hundreds of different flavors, our tongues register just five basic tastes. (If I had my way, I'd add a sixth taste to the list—freshness. Though it's hard to describe, without it the other five don't mean nearly as much!) When we eat, our thousands of taste buds—tiny cells plugged into nerve endings on our tongues—send instant signals to our brains, contributing to the overall sensation of flavor. The five tastes we are able to discern are:

Sweet. If you have a powerful sweet tooth, you're not alone! Many of us (myself included) have an innate preference for sweet foods—that is, we naturally crave sweet tastes. The good news is that white sugar, high fructose corn syrup, and other unhealthy, refined ingredients are far from the only sources of sweetness available to us. Fruit sugars, some alcohols, and even spices like cinnamon all taste sweet—giving us plenty of options for satisfying our craving healthfully.

Sour. The puckering reaction we have to acidic foods such as vinegar, cranberries, citrus fruits, and even some vegetables (such as rhubarb) may seem unpleasant on its own. But sour notes can add complexity to a recipe and help balance out other flavors; and a mild tart taste can create a sensation of refreshment, as in a lemon sorbet.

Salty. Sodium chloride—table salt—is the most common source of salty sensation. Salt can enhance natural flavors and balance other spices, but it can also dominate our palates, so that we fail to notice other, subtler tastes. Reducing salt will not only open up a whole new world of flavor, it will also help boost overall health: Limiting sodium intake is an important way to control high blood pressure. This doesn't mean we need to ban it from our kitchens. But learning how to coax the most flavor out of your ingredients allows you to cut back on the amount of salt you need to add to your food.

Bitter. Our ability to sense bitterness may have originally helped our prehistoric ancestors avoid plants full of poisonous alkaloids. While we still tend to avoid extremely bitter foods, there are plenty of milder variations of this taste sensation we've learned to enjoy—our morning cup of coffee and evening glass of wine both have bitter notes, for example. Grapefruit skin and tonic water (which contains bitter quinine) are other sources we tolerate of this taste sensation.

Savory (umami). A relative newcomer to the roster of five basic tastes, *umami,* a Japanese word that translates as "savory" or "meaty," was identified in the early 1900s and has been gaining in popularity in recent years. The rich, silky taste is associated with glutamate, originally found in seaweed used to make soup in Japan but also found in soup stocks, mushrooms, and many other foods that have prominent places in the *Flavor First* pantry. Yeast extracts (available in health food stores) can also be used to boost the umami taste—and are a healthy way to add richness without slathering dishes with fats.

Smell

When it comes to experiencing food flavors, we rely even more on smell than on taste—a fact that's most evident when you're suffering from a cold or nasal congestion and everything you eat tastes bland. While your tongue registers just five basic tastes, the millions of olfactory cells in your nose can discern among hundreds of nuanced odors that contribute to your overall experience of flavor.

It's generally recognized that the complex aromas we smell are made up of varying combinations of different scents. But because so many smells exist, scientists haven't settled on a precise list of basic odors on which all others are based, the way they have with taste.

For the purposes of creating flavorful food, though, it's useful to consider these "classes" of odors. Some, such as musk, may not sound appetizing in and of themselves, but remember it's very rare that you smell any of these scents individually. You generally perceive a subtle symphony of odors—such as the mouthwatering aroma of a favorite spaghetti sauce—that may contain a combination of all the classes below.

Floral. These heady aromas are usually associated with sweets and fruits.

Mint. This refreshing aroma can brighten everything from salads to meats to desserts.

Musk. Some meat dishes have a mild musky odor that can add to an overall impression of richness. Meat stews often emit a slightly earthy, sharp odor that contrasts well with herbs and spices.

Pungent. Your favorite blue cheese has the tang that balances beautifully with everything from crisp salads to sweet pears. Anchovies, fermented foods such as Korean kimchi, and even cooked asparagus and broccoli can have pungent odors.

Smoky/burnt. Grilled meats and fire-roasted tomatoes are among the foods that can take on added complexity with notes of smoke or charring.

Camphor. This sharp scent can evoke a medicinal aroma or, more pleasantly, eucalyptus or pine. Black cardamom lends a subtle whiff of camphor to dishes, while camphor itself is used as a seasoning in some Indian desserts.

Touch

The sense of touch as experienced against your tongue and in your mouth is called texture or mouthfeel, and it's an important component of flavor. We associate silky textures with richness, for example, even if little fat is present. If a food is tough and fibrous, by contrast, we may decide it's unpleasant to eat, even if it's sweet. Most people would prefer to savor a spoonful of creamy chocolate, for example, as opposed to gnawing on a tough stalk of sugarcane.

The sensations that make up mouthfeel include:

Pain. Some peppers literally stimulate pain receptors in your mouth—a sensation we register as spicy heat when it's mild, but which can be unpleasant if too intense. Many people *love* this feeling!

Temperature. Hot foods can provide comfort on a winter's day, while a crisp, cool salad can refresh in midsummer. But flavors are more pronounced when at a moderate temperature, between 68° and 86°F. Foods that are frozen solid, like ice cream, need stronger flavoring to make an impact, which is why melted ice cream tends to taste too sweet.

Astringency. Astringency causes a puckering sensation on your tongue. The tannins in tea or red wine cause an astringent sensation, as do some citrus flavors.

Smoothness. The silky mouthfeel we associate with creamy sauces and drinks contributes to a sensation of richness.

Crispness. The satisfying crunch of a perfectly ripe apple or the snap of a stalk of celery is an important part of our enjoyment.

Chewiness. Foods that give our teeth and jaws a workout can be pleasurable—such as a slice of thick, crusty bread—or we can identify the sensation as undesirable, as in tough, stringy, or overcooked meat.

Density. A serving of thickly layered veggie lasagna feels heartier and more satisfying than the same size portion of steamed vegetables served over fluffy rice. You can satisfy cravings for comfort food healthfully by eating dense, substantial foods that are low in fat and starch.

With a nearly infinite number of combinations of taste, aroma, and texture at your fingertips, the range of flavors you can create is endless. By experimenting with different flavor profiles, you will build a repertoire of healthy, nutrient-rich dishes that enliven all of your senses.

FLAVOR AROUND THE GLOBE

One way to begin exploring new flavors is to take a virtual trip around the globe. Civilizations throughout history have adapted their cuisines to the logistics of the environment in which they lived—the geography, the climate, and the indigenous plants and animals available to them. As inhabitants of the 21st century, most of us can sample the world's cuisines without ever having to venture farther than a short drive from home—a luxury that radically expands our flavor options.

Here are just a few of the regional cuisines that have influenced the recipes in *Flavor First*.

Northern Asia

Chinese cuisine encompasses a range of regional styles. Dishes from southern China emphasize freshness and tenderness, while in the colder north, dishes are oilier, and pungent vinegar- and garlic-based flavorings are more popular. Noodles and rice are used as a starchy base for protein and vegetables, or as a side dish.

Like Chinese cuisine, Japanese dishes emphasize the use of vegetables in balance with meat, poultry, and fish. Light and subtle flavorings such as miso and rice vinegar put the emphasis on fresh (or often raw) ingredients, spotlighting the high quality and variety of seasonal produce and seafood native to this island nation. The emphasis on vegetables and fish makes the Japanese diet one of the healthiest on earth: Japanese people have the lowest obesity rate in the developed world, according to the International Obesity Taskforce. And Okinawa boasts the largest population of centenarians anywhere, thanks in large part to their healthy food choices and active lifestyle.

In both Chinese and Japanese cuisines, soy sauce, ginger, and garlic are dominant seasonings, while the Japanese were the first to identify the sensation of umami.

Southeast Asia

In Thailand, Vietnam, Indonesia, and other countries in Southeast Asia, traditional dishes are aromatic and rely on a bounty of herbs, spices, and sauces that are now easier than ever to source at your local grocery store. Citrus juices, basil, cilantro, and mint are frequently used to flavor foods, while condiments like fish sauce add still more zest.

Generally, Southeast Asian dishes are prepared using quick-cooking methods—such as stir-frying or steaming—that preserve the freshness of the ingredients. Fragrant soups such as Vietnamese *pho* take a bit longer to cook but provide an entire meal in a bowl—full of fresh seafood, crisp-tender vegetables, and savory thick noodles.

India

A cornucopia of spices is cultivated in India—from exotic flavors such as cardamom and turmeric to more familiar spices like cinnamon and black pepper—and as a result, Indian cuisine takes advantage of a wider range of spices than almost any other world cuisine.

Curries are a popular staple in India, but unlike Southeast Asian curries, which are based on high-fat coconut milk, Indian curries typically use yogurt as a base, making them a more nutritious option. And because there's a strong tradition of vegetarianism in the Hindu religion, vegetables are a focus of Indian cuisine, making it a rich source for healthy recipes.

Latin America

When Spanish conquistadors arrived in Mexico and South America in the 16th century, they quickly appropriated an entire hemisphere of new flavors and ingredients, from chocolate to chile peppers. They also found a new, protein-rich grain rumored to have fueled ancient Inca warriors' greatest feats. Today we know this nutrient-dense miracle seed as quinoa.

Today's Latin American cuisine is the resulting blend of these native influences with European culinary traditions. While the fare served at many fast-food-style "Mexican" restaurants—with its heavy emphasis on cheese, nachos, and deep-fried foods—isn't exactly low calorie, traditional Mexican food makes use of healthy, flavorful ingredients such as fresh vegetable salsas, avocados, baked corn tortillas, spicy bean dishes, and healthy proteins.

The Mediterranean

Though more than 15 countries border the Mediterranean Sea—each with its own unique cuisine and regional variations, from Casablanca to the Amalfi Coast—the region's mild climate has created commonalities in diet that transcend national boundaries. The all-inclusive term *Mediterranean diet,* which has become popular in recent years, refers to a heart-healthy and nutritious diet high in fruits, vegetables, whole grains, and fresh seafood. Olive oil is the primary source of dietary fat in Mediterranean dishes, and rich sources of protein such as red meat are considered special-occasion fare.

From Spanish paella to stuffed grape leaves, many of this region's dishes may already be among your favorites. Once you learn how to create the distinctive flavors of the Mediterranean, you'll be able to cook a wide range of healthy, delicious, and authentic dishes.

COOKING UP HEALTHY FLAVOR

Now that you've experienced a taste of how cultures around the world approach flavor, you're probably wondering how to translate these global influences into your own kitchen. In the pages that follow, you'll find an overview of the basics you need to know. Once you master these concepts, you'll be able to create any flavor profile you desire.

Freshness equals flavor. Regardless of the recipe, the quality of the outcome is a function of the quality of the ingredients you use. Buy the freshest, highest-quality foods you can afford. Depending on your budget, it's not always possible to buy organic produce and prime-grade fish, poultry, and meats. But on the other hand, once you're comfortable experimenting with a variety of flavors and styles, you may discover you're dining out less without losing out on flavor—which can result in substantial savings. Similarly, focusing your diet on "clean"

foods made from fresh, whole ingredients is likely to be more filling and satisfying than consuming an abundance of processed foods; you may find you need less of the good stuff and achieve savings through quality over quantity.

A few more tips to help maximize your fresh-food dollar:

Buy seasonal and local produce. Although our expansive modern supermarkets stock produce year-round, many items travel thousands of miles to reach the shelves. To keep costs down—both yours and the environment's—try visiting a local farmers' market and acquainting yourself with what's available seasonally. You'll find that not only is the produce a better value, but it tastes better, too. See the Shopping Sources section on page 199 for information on how to find a farmers' market near you.

Shop more frequently and buy less food. There's nothing worse than buying lots of tantalizing produce, only to have it spoil before you have a chance to use it all. If you're used to shopping once a week or less, you may find it's best to add a midweek shopping trip to your schedule so you can buy produce in smaller quantities and avoid waste.

Get to know your butcher and fishmonger. If you're used to buying prepackaged meats, poultry, and fish, it can be intimidating to step up to the meat counter and ask questions. But butchers and fishmongers are extremely knowledgeable resources and offer a wealth of information about the most flavorful cuts of meat and which fish are most plentiful now (and hence cost less)—so ask away! They're also usually happy to debone your meats and remove the skin from your fish fillets, saving you valuable time in the kitchen. And you may be surprised by some of the valuable cooking tips they have to offer!

Grow your own. You don't have to own a farm to grow your own herbs. All you need is a sunny windowsill and a few flower pots to start your own patch of basil, rosemary, or thyme. Not only will you save money on buying fresh herbs, but you'll also be able to snip off just what you need instead of buying a big bunch that you'll never be able to use up. If you have a little more room outside, consider planting a few of your favorite vegetables—the flavor of tomatoes or snap peas right off the vine is unparalleled. And the satisfaction of growing, cooking, and eating your own food is well worth the investment of time and resources.

Use salt properly. Unlike herbs and spices, which derive from plants, salt is a dietary mineral extracted from the earth or from seawater. Most salt today is mined from the shores of dry salt lakes or inlets.

Salt is our top source of sodium, an essential component of our diets that helps regulate fluid levels in our bodies. But because salt is so pervasive—used not only as a seasoning in savory dishes but also as a preservative in processed foods—many of us ingest too much of it, causing an imbalance in body fluids that can lead to high blood pressure. We need only about 2.4 grams of sodium per day—about the amount contained in a single teaspoon of table salt—but most of us eat far more, as much as twice that amount, according to some estimates. For that reason, many recipes in this book use minimal added salt; if you're on a sodium-restricted diet, you can eliminate it altogether. *Flavor First* recipes can be easily adjusted to your seasoning preferences.

If you do use salt, try experimenting with several varieties to achieve different results, depending on the dish you're making. Here's a run-down of a few of the options available to you.

- **Sea salt.** Again, the name says it all. This type of salt isn't mined, but rather extracted from seawater through the time-consuming process of evaporation, making it more expensive than table or kosher salt. It is available in fine-grained or chunkier crystals; depending on the grain, you may want to use a grinder or a mortar and pestle to achieve the consistency you want. Conventional varieties of sea salt are refined and may contain additives, just like table salt; if you're after absolute purity, be sure to read the label.

- **Table salt.** This fine-grained salt is inexpensive and easy to pour; it's mined and then refined into sugar-size granules. Iodized salt is a type of table salt that's fortified with iodine, an essential element that supports thyroid function.

- **Kosher salt.** As the name implies, this salt is used in the process of koshering meat in accordance with Jewish dietary guidelines. Kosher salt dissolves more easily than table salt and is favored by many cooks for its light, flaky texture.

At right: A variety of salts. Counterclockwise from the top: sea salt, table salt, kosher salt, flavored salt, and rock salt.

- **Flavored salt.** Flavored or seasoned salts are simply table salt blended with other herbs and vegetable extracts. Often it's better to use the herbs and vegetables themselves—chopped garlic rather than garlic salt, for example, imparts a fresher, more pure garlic flavor without the added sodium. But some recipes do benefit greatly from the flavor of seasoned salts. Making them yourself is easy (and much less expensive) than buying fancy blends. See pages 193 to 195 for recipes.

- **Rock salt.** Even chunkier than sea salt, this unrefined salt is grayish in color and is used primarily as a decorative bed for serving seafood such as oysters or shrimp. It can also be used in your hand-cranked ice cream maker.

Incorporate herbs and spices. Even small amounts of herbs and spices deliver a powerful punch of flavor. In addition, many herbs and spices are loaded with antioxidants—substances that help protect your body from diseases such as heart disease and cancer. The table on page 14 shows the ORAC (oxygen radical absorbance capacity) values of various herbs and spices. The higher the number, the more potent the antioxidant punch.

Like antioxidant-rich vegetables and fruits, herbs and spices derive from plants. An herb is usually made from leafy plant material, while spices can come from any other part of the plant, from roots to fruits, although most are made from seeds. Generally, spices grow in tropical climates, while herbs grow in more temperate regions—although some plants deliver both. The leaves of the cilantro plant, for example, are used as an herb, while its seeds are made into the spice, coriander seed.

A handful of plant families provide the bulk of our herbs and spices:

The mint family (Lamiaceae). Largely consisting of plants native to Mediterranean climates, this family is the source of our most familiar herbs. Among them:

- **Oregano.** The popular pizza flavoring has a warm, slightly bitter taste.

- **Peppermint and spearmint.** Both plants have a refreshing menthol taste used in everything from cocktails to candies.

- **Basil.** This fresh, vegetal herb is best known as the base ingredient for pesto.

- **Rosemary.** The leaves of this evergreen shrub have a piney appearance and impart a woody, rich flavor that's popular in autumn and winter dishes.

- **Sage.** This slightly peppery herb is perfect for marinades.

- **Thyme.** With a slightly lemony, vegetal flavor, thyme is an excellent accompaniment to seafood.

At right: The mint family.
From left to right: oregano,
spearmint, basil, rosemary,
sage, thyme, and peppermint.

The carrot family (Apiaceae). In addition to carrots, celery, and other vegetables, this family includes a number of plants that are rich in essential oils and flavor. They include:

- **Coriander/cilantro.** A warm flavor with citrus overtones, coriander seed is also a popular spice for Indian dishes. The leaves of the same plant, cilantro, have a flavor that some find too "soapy" for their liking. Cilantro is added to many Mexican dishes for a note of freshness.

- **Anise and fennel.** Both herbs have a licorice flavor; the slightly spicy, crunchy bulb of the fennel plant is typically sliced thin and consumed raw in salads.

- **Parsley.** This leafy herb adds a fresh note to virtually any dish. Chopped parsley is often sprinkled on food just prior to serving. Curly and Italian parsley are common varieties.

- **Cumin.** The warm, sharp aromas of this distinctive spice are popular in Indian cuisine and can also add tang to soups, fish dishes, and even some gingerbread recipes.

At left: The carrot family.
Clockwise from the top:
parsley, cumin, cilantro,
coriander, and fennel.

The ginger family (Zingiberaceae). Native to southern Asia, these plants give us warm flavors that lend an exotic perfume to everyday dishes.

- **Cardamom.** This warm, slightly astringent, citrusy spice is used in Indian spice mixtures such as garam masala and is also found in northern European sweet pastries and breads. In Middle Eastern culture, it's a familiar scent in many households, where it's steeped daily for tea.

- **Ginger.** When used fresh, the root of this plant is both refreshingly pungent and spicy, adding distinctive zing to beverages, soups, poultry, and fish. Dried and crushed to a powder, ginger is a popular flavor for baked goods.

The mustard family (Brassicaceae). This family is the source of many hot, biting flavors, including:

- **Mustard.** The seeds of the mustard plant are crushed and made into the popular condiment we spread on sandwiches and eat with a variety of meats, adding pungency and spice.

- **Horseradish.** The roots of a plant (*Armoracia lapathifolia*) are crushed to produce this zesty component of cocktail sauce that also lends its heat to a variety of dips and spreads.

The pepper family (Piperaceae). The best-known species in this family of flowering plants is the vine that produces pepper seeds (or peppercorns), which account for one-quarter of all spice production worldwide. White pepper is produced from a different species of plant and generally has a milder flavor than black pepper.

HERBS AND SPICES: THE ORAC SCORE

The ORAC scale is used to quantify the antioxidant potency of foods. The higher the score, the higher the antioxidant capacity of the food.

SPICES	ORAC PER ½ TSP
Cloves, ground	3,144
Cinnamon, ground	2,675
Turmeric	1,593
Curry powder	485
Black pepper, whole peppercorns	451
Mustard seed, ground	440
Chili powder	354
Ginger, ground	288
Black pepper, ground	251
Paprika	179
Garlic powder	101
Onion powder	57
Poppy seed	8
HERBS	ORAC PER ½ TSP
Oregano, dried	1,334
Tarragon, fresh	933
Oregano, fresh	838
Thyme, fresh	658
Marjoram, fresh	655
Sage, fresh	641
Basil, dried	338
Basil, fresh	127
Parsley, dried	124
Peppermint, fresh	87
Parsley, fresh	49
Dill, fresh	25
Rosemary, fresh	6
Chives, fresh	3

The chile pepper family (Solanaceae). The plant family that includes both potatoes and nightshade is the source of habaneros, poblanos, jalapeños, and other types of spicy chile peppers, as well as milder bell peppers. Latin and Mexican dishes often use sliced, crushed, or diced chiles, while Italian recipes sometimes call for a roasted hot pepper or a dash of spicy dried hot pepper flakes to add subtle heat to tomato-based sauces.

The onion family (Alliaceae). In addition to the pungent vegetable that adds flavor to so many dishes, the onion family includes garlic, a potent source of flavor for many cuisines around the world. Chopped garlic can be sautéed with a wide variety of ingredients for an extra kick of flavor; roasting garlic in the oven creates a milder, almost nutty flavor that complements poultry, meats, and rich sauces. Shallots and chives are also members of the onion family.

As you expand your ingredient repertoire, you'll also expand your repertoire of flavor. There are literally hundreds of herbs and spices to explore; for additional information on how to source them, consult page 202 in the Shopping Sources at the back of this book.

Oils

When we think about how to add flavor to food, we usually turn to seasonings like salt, herbs, and spices. But there's a whole other category of ingredients that contribute to a dish's taste: fats. Although fat has long been the villain of the weight-loss industry, it's important to understand that the right kinds of fats are a key component of a healthy diet.

Fat gets its bad reputation from the fact that it is high in calories, and because some fats—such as the saturated fats found in meat and whole-milk dairy products, and the trans fats found in many processed and fried foods—can increase artery-blocking LDL ("bad") cholesterol and contribute to heart disease and high blood pressure. But the unsaturated fats found in vegetable and seed oils actually offer health benefits; they not only lower LDL counts but boost levels of HDL, the "good" cholesterol that helps evacuate LDL via the liver. As with all calorie-dense foods, moderation is key when it comes to fat. It should account for no more than 25 percent of your daily caloric intake, especially if you're trying to lose weight.

As any food chemist can tell you, many flavor compounds are fat soluble. This means that knowing how to use healthy oils in your cooking can actually make your food taste more robust, because these good fats act as flavor carriers. Different varieties of oil can impart very different flavors, and their fat content adds richness to a dish and promotes a feeling of satiety, or fullness, when you eat it—a good thing when you're trying to lose weight.

The recipes in this book make use of a variety of healthy oils, each of which contributes its own unique flavor to a dish. Most of these oils are versatile enough to be used both in dressings and vinaigrettes and in cooked dishes, as they have a high "smoke point"—that is, they can withstand high temperatures before they begin to smoke and turn acrid. There are two main categories of healthy oils: vegetable oils, including seed oils, and nut oils.

Seed oils. A subset of vegetable oils, seed oils are made from pressed plant seeds and deliver highly concentrated nutrients and flavors in small doses. Seed oils used in this book include:

■ **Canola oil.** Derived from a variety of rapeseed plant, this is the go-to oil in my kitchen, as it is low in saturated fats and high in omega-3s, has a high smoke point, and lends a neutral taste to foods that allows the flavors of the main ingredients to take center stage.

■ **Flaxseed oil.** Containing heart-healthy omega-3 fatty acids, this oil is mild enough to be used in salad dressings, although its low smoke point makes it undesirable for cooking.

■ **Grapeseed oil.** This slightly nutty oil has antioxidant properties and withstands heat well. It can be infused with herbs to create an aromatic oil for salads.

■ **Sesame oil.** Both the light and dark varieties of this oil are extracted from sesame seeds; the darker variety lends a pronounced nutty flavor to dishes. A common ingredient in Asian cooking, sesame oil has a high smoke point, which makes it a popular option for stir-frying. Sesame oil is high in polyunsaturated fats.

Vegetable oils. These oils are extracted from plant matter. They include:

■ **Olive oil.** This staple of the Mediterranean diet has been used since 3000 BC and has a slightly grassy, vegetal flavor. "Extra-virgin" and "virgin" oils come from the first pressings and are unrefined; their flavors are purest for salad dressings and other uncooked sauces. Lower grades (such as "semi-fine" or "pure") are less flavorful but withstand high temperatures better. Olive oil contains not only HDL-boosting compounds but also vitamin E and antioxidants.

■ **Soybean oil.** The light yellow oil extracted from soybeans is often used in margarine and many of the all-purpose cooking oils available in supermarkets. This neutral-tasting oil is high in both polyunsaturated and monounsaturated fats, is low in saturated fats, and contains omega-3 fatty acids.

Nut oils. Like the nuts from which they're produced, nut oils are a good source of beneficial fats. Nut oils tend to be pricier than vegetable oils, so they come in smaller bottles. It's worth investing in a few good-quality nut oils, which will add flavor and healthy fats to your dishes. Two of the nut oils I often use are:

■ **Walnut oil.** This oil has a delicate flavor and is high in omega-3 fatty acids, which promote heart and brain health. It's ideal for salads but doesn't hold up well when heated to high temperatures.

■ **Almond oil.** Almost as low in saturated fats as canola oil, this aromatic oil has a higher smoke point than walnut oil, making it more versatile for use in cooking.

Vinegars and Other Liquid Flavor Agents

Fermentation is the chemical process that creates some of our favorite grown-up beverages, from crisp white wines to hearty ales. But fermentation is also an ally when it comes to flavor: It's the method by which a number of tart, zingy condiments are created.

We usually think of vinegar as a counterpoint to oil in salad dressings. But this pantry staple—whose name comes from the French term *vin aigre,* or "sour wine"—can lend its tart, astringent flavor to an array of dishes, from soups to desserts.

While distilled white vinegar is the most common variety you'll find, it's also the least flavorful. Try experimenting with the following vinegars to add more robust flavor to your dishes:

Balsamic vinegar. Made from Italian white wine grapes, this luscious dark vinegar is often sweet enough to enjoy on salads without adding oil. Reducing it to a syrup is a quick and easy way to create a sauce that is delicious with fruit.

Malt vinegar. This mild vinegar is best known as an accompaniment to fish and chips but can add zip to vegetable sautés and other dishes as well.

Rice vinegar. A staple in Asian cooking, this extremely mild vinegar adds sweet notes to salad dressings. It is available in seasoned and unseasoned varieties; I recommend using the unseasoned vinegar.

Apple cider vinegar. This sweet, fruity vinegar can be used to impart flavor to meat marinades and salads.

Vinegar also forms the base for another popular condiment: hot pepper sauce, most commonly known by the brand name Tabasco. Made from vinegar, hot peppers, and salt, hot sauce is commonly used in Latin dishes, and a few shakes can transform scrambled eggs from ordinary to olé!

While vinegars tend to add sharpness and bite to a dish, other fermented condiments contribute rich umami flavors. Because they make foods taste rich without added fat, these condiments are especially useful—but be sure to check the labels, as these sauces tend to contain a lot of salt. Choose low-sodium versions when available.

Soy sauce. This nutty liquid is made from fermented soybeans and barley or wheat, and is a key flavoring in Asian dishes. Most supermarkets carry dark soy sauce from Japan, but lighter, milder

WHEN TO ADD FLAVOR

You probably know that it's important to follow recipe instructions carefully, especially when preparing a dish for the first time. But in addition to accurately following the basic steps of preparation, it's also crucial to add the herbs and spices in the order directed.

The flavors of herbs and spices derive from their essential oils, which diminish over time in dried or powdered form. If you freshly grind whole spices or chop fresh herbs, their newly released essential oils will make the flavors more potent than store-bought dried or powdered herbs and spices. Add freshly chopped and ground herbs and spices later in the cooking process to ensure their flavors don't overwhelm the other ingredients. Whole herbs and spices, such as bay leaves, release their flavor slowly and should be added at the beginning of cooking (and removed before serving!).

THE RAW TRUTH

In recent years, the raw food movement, which advocates eating exclusively uncooked foods, has gained popularity. Raw fruits and vegetables are outstanding sources of both nutrients and flavors—from crisp apples to brightly colored bell peppers. Even some meats and fish can be enjoyed raw, in preparations like carpaccio, tartare, and sushi.

But while cooking can reduce the amounts of water-soluble antioxidants (such as vitamins B and C) present in fresh fruits and vegetables, it also can increase the concentration of fat-soluble antioxidants—carotenoids such as lycopene (found in tomatoes) and lutein (found in broccoli, brussels sprouts, and spinach). A 2002 Cornell University study found that the antioxidant properties of tomatoes increase as much as 35 percent when cooked!

Just as a healthy diet employs a balanced approach to nutrients, so should your cooking incorporate a balanced mix of raw and cooked fruits and vegetables. Let great flavor be your guide; after all, the more delicious your vegetable and fruit preparations, the more tempting they'll be to eat. Establishing this habit is key to a healthy diet.

---

varieties are also available—look in your local ethnic foods market or online for different kinds of soy sauce. The amino acids in soy transform with fermentation into the slick, salty umami taste.

Tamari. Like soy sauce, tamari is made from soybeans, but it has a milder flavor and slightly thicker texture. True tamari is fermented without wheat—making it a gluten-free alternative to soy sauce—but because the term *tamari* is sometimes used to describe and market various types of soy sauce, be sure to read the label if you have a gluten allergy.

Fish sauce. Another source of umami, fish sauce is made from the liquid collected from fermented fish. The sauce has the tang of seaweed and a strong fishy taste.

Worcestershire sauce. Originally a variant of fish sauce, Worcestershire is made from a vinegar base. Current versions of this tangy sauce can still contain anchovies, along with soy sauce, garlic, and other spices. Worcestershire sauce is used to flavor meats, gravies, and soups—not to mention Bloody Mary cocktails.

In Chapter 10, you'll find recipes for making your own healthy, flavorful condiments, including dressings, marinades, and spreads. But with these basic staples stocked in your pantry, you're ready to boost flavor at a moment's notice.

FLAVORFUL PREPARATIONS

Adding herbs, spices, oils, and vinegars to your foods is one way to create flavor. Another simple way to impart great taste is through your choice of cooking method. The way you prepare food expands your options for flavor; the ultimate taste of a dish is determined by how it is cooked.

When it comes to preparing healthy meals, many experts advise you to steam or boil your food. While these methods certainly don't add fat or calories to your ingredients, they also don't add much flavor. But it can be easy to fall into a rut and fall back on the same old cooking methods we know and trust, especially when we're pressured for time and want to stick to what's "safe" for our weight-loss or nutrition goals. The good news is that there are many flavorful cooking methods that don't rely on added fat for flavor—and they're just as easy to prepare as your old standbys. In fact, they may even save you time in the kitchen!

I urge you to try out one new preparation method each week to ease yourself into a new repertoire of culinary skills. You'll be surprised at how quickly your menu options expand—and how easy it is to add flavor without fuss.

Precooking Prep: Baths, Rubs, and More

No, we're not talking about spa treatments! But the following methods will create flavors that feel just as decadent, before you even fire up a burner or preheat the oven.

Marinade (or wet rub). Soaking meat, fish, or vegetables in a bath of aromatic liquid prior to cooking is one way to add flavor. Typically consisting of an acidic substance like lemon juice or red wine, plus oil and other herbs, a marinade softens the texture of some ingredients and infuses them with flavor—although there's little evidence that the liquid soaks in much farther than $\frac{1}{4}$ inch. The more surface area is exposed, the greater the tenderizing effect of the marinade, making it ideal for spicing up kebabs for the grill. The soaking time will depend on the size and amount of ingredients to marinate as well as what goes into the liquid itself—generally, the more acidic the marinade, the less soaking time is needed. Too much time in an acidic marinade will break down the protein of meats and change the texture, so it's important to strike the right balance.

If you plan to serve the marinade as a dipping sauce or dressing, discard any portions that were used for bathing raw fish or meat, and always refrigerate foods as they marinate to prevent the growth of harmful bacteria.

Brine. Just as marinades rely on acid to create the desired texture and flavor, brines rely on another seasoning ingredient: salt. Completely submerging and soaking meats in an extremely salty solution for an extended period of time—roughly 1 hour per pound, depending on meat density—gives them a tender, juicy texture and a salty flavor that goes well with smoking or grilling preparations.

The obvious downside of brining is that it imparts a lot of salt to your food. You can reduce the sodium content of brined foods by rinsing them just after brining and before cooking.

Dry rub. In contrast with a marinade, a dry rub contains no liquid; instead, herbs and spices are mixed together, sometimes with a mashed garlic or onion paste, and then spread (or rubbed)

A FRENCH FLAVOR SECRET: THE BOUQUET GARNI

French cooks infuse rich flavor into soups, sauces, and braised meats by adding a sachet of herbs known as a bouquet garni, which typically contains parsley, bay leaf, and thyme. It's easy to make your own bouquet garni: Simply bundle together a few sprigs or leaves of each herb with kitchen twine, tie tightly, and toss into your pot. Remove and discard the bouquet prior to serving. *Voilà!* Instant flavor.

---

by hand onto meat, poultry, or fish to form a flavorful crust. Fat-free and intensely flavorful, this method is great for foods you plan to put on the grill or rotisserie.

Tenderize. While soaking meat in an acidic marinade is one way to make it less chewy, you can achieve the same effect through somewhat rougher means. Think of tenderizing as tough love for tough cuts of meat: Using a wooden or metal mallet, you literally pound meat to break down its fibers. You can also slice or grind meat to achieve the desired texture. You may find this step unnecessary if you buy your meats already sliced or ground—but if you want to get in a good upper-body workout while cooking, tenderizing is the method for you!

COOKING UP FLAVOR

Once you've prepped your ingredients, it's time to get cooking. When you cook food, you apply heat to it in one of two ways: dry heat or wet heat. Dry heat methods surround your ingredients—whether in your oven or on a grill—with hot, dry air. When cooking with dry heat, use nonstick cookware to avoid adding fat as a lubricant, and set the stove or oven to the correct temperature to ensure foods retain flavor and cook within the time frame that will produce the best results. Wet heat methods use hot liquid—such as water or broth—to cook food. The food can be fully or partially submerged, or even suspended over the liquid. Cooking with water or flavorful broth eliminates the need for added fat.

Each of the following dry- and wet-heat techniques will add flavor to your dishes without relying on added oils or other fats.

Dry-Heat Cooking Methods

Baking. Most people think of baking in conjunction with making sweets and desserts—but baking is a great way to cook savory dishes as well. Though we've all experienced the unpleasant textures (dryness, chewiness) and flavors that result from overbaking, perfectly baked food retains just the right amount of moisture and optimal flavor development. Baking requires that you cook food in an oven at a steady temperature, usually between 200° and 400°F. Because the cooking temperature is typically on the low end of that scale, baking often

HEALTHY GRILLING

Sometimes during grilling or broiling, your food gets too close to the flame and becomes partially charred. While some people love this "burned" taste, charring can create dangerous carcinogens. To grill and broil your food healthfully:

■ Drain and blot away any excess oil after marinating.

■ Place your food on foil or a grill topper to prevent fat from dripping onto the coals or gas burners.

■ Cut away any portion of food that becomes blackened during cooking.

requires more time than other dry-heat methods. When you bake foods, the air circulating around the pan is what cooks the food—so if you bake multiple dishes at once, expect the baking time to increase.

Broiling. Similar to baking, broiling is a technique used to cook foods in the oven at a high temperature. Broiled foods develop a distinctive flavor based on the caramelization of sugar that occurs when foods are heated at a high temperature. The food needs to be placed directly beneath a heat source, such as an open flame or the top heating element in your oven, usually at temperatures above 450°F. Foods cook quickly under the broiler, so be sure to monitor your dish carefully to avoid burning.

Grilling. Grilled foods are cooked directly above a heat source, which can be a stove-top grill or grill pan, or an outdoor grill. Like broiling, this method browns and crisps the exterior of foods and depending on the heat source can add a smoky flavor, too. Although used interchangeably with the term *barbecue,* there's a difference—grilling is a quick cooking method using high temperatures over an open heat source, while

barbecuing consists of cooking foods for long periods at lower temperatures in an enclosed cooking device, such as a pit or a smoker.

Roasting. Like baking, roasting uses the dry heat of an oven to cook foods. But while baked foods can be cooked in a variety of vessels, roasted foods are specifically cooked in an open pan. This method adds depth to flavor and richness to vegetables, poultry, fish, and meats. Be sure not to crowd the pan when roasting several smaller foods—like vegetables or chicken breasts; it's important to allow the hot air to circulate around each item so that all can brown and cook evenly. Low temperatures are used for roasting larger foods, such as a whole chicken. High-temperature roasting is used for smaller foods, such as vegetables, potatoes, or small pieces of meat or fish. A combination method is sometimes used with roasted meats to quickly brown or sear them at high heat and then reduce the heat to low for slow roasting and a moist and flavorful end result.

Toasting. This method requires that you quickly heat and brown the surface of a food by placing it near a heat source. Toasting is a great way to add crunch—think croutons in soup or on salad—and can add depth of flavor to spices, grains, and nuts and seeds (such as cumin, almonds, or flaked coconut).

Wet-Heat Cooking Methods

Boiling. This is probably one of the most commonly used cooking methods in the everyday repertoire. Food cooked by this method is immersed in boiling-hot liquid (often water). Because the boiling point of most liquids is 212°F, foods that are boiled never get hot enough to brown. We tend to associate boiled foods with blandness, but if you use vegetable or chicken stock rather than water as the base liquid, you'll instantly boost flavor. You can also add a bouquet garni (see page 21) or spice sachet to the boiling liquid, and the food in the pot will take on the aromatic flavor of those herbs or spices. Think of boiling as an opportunity to bathe foods in a flavorful soup.

Poaching. A variant of boiling, poaching involves cooking food in a small amount of boiling water (or another liquid), usually just enough to cover the food being poached. The liquid can be seasoned for extra flavor. Although many specialized poaching pans exist, a shallow saucepan or skillet works well; use a slotted spoon to remove the poached food when done. When you poach delicate foods such as eggs or fish fillets, be sure to keep the water at a gentle—not rolling—boil.

Pressure cooking. A pressure cooker is a heavy pot with a very tight-fitting lid that creates a seal, allowing pressure to build up inside the pot when it's placed over heat. This method cooks food more quickly, thereby drastically reducing preparation time.

Steaming. To steam food, it must be suspended over boiling liquid in a covered pot. The steam produced from the liquid below circulates around the food and cooks it through. Instead of using plain water to steam your foods, you can create more flavor by adding aromatic herbs, spices, or even tea leaves to the pot.

Stewing. Another variation on boiling, stewing involves covering food with a bare minimum of liquid and cooking it gently for a long period of time in a covered pot. Cooking a dish slowly over low heat allows the flavor of all the ingredients to blend together, infusing the liquid with richness and depth of flavor.

There are also a few "in between" cooking methods that don't fall squarely into either wet or dry cooking categories. These are also great ways to add flavor to your dish.

Braising. Browning ingredients by roasting, baking, or grilling them, then cooking them in a small amount of liquid will help your food retain moisture. Braised foods are typically cooked in a covered pot or pan. Unlike stewing, the ingredients aren't completely covered by liquid; rather, just enough liquid is used to create steam and keep moisture circulating. The result is a tender, juicy dish with rich flavor similar to that of a roast.

Sautéing. The word *sauté* comes from the French verb *sauter,* which means "to jump." This method involves cooking ingredients in a shallow pan over high heat and intermittently shaking the pan to make the food "jump." To minimize the use of fat, opt for a nonstick pan coated with just a mist of oil.

Microwaving. Cooking food in the microwave oven uses neither hot air nor hot liquid, but electromagnetic radiation. In a microwave oven, radiation cooks food swiftly without requiring fat, but ingredients often lose moisture (and change texture) in the process. And because ingredients are cooked evenly throughout, microwaved foods don't brown. I use my microwave mostly to heat milk for my coffee or to warm up frozen foods or leftovers.

KITCHEN ESSENTIALS FOR FLAVORFUL COOKING

A few basic kitchen implements will save you time and effort in the kitchen. Here's a list of the essential gadgets you need to create the recipes in this book and many other healthy, flavorful dishes. While the recipes in this book all use standard measuring cup and spoon measurements, the chart on the opposite page will come in handy when you need to convert measurements for various recipes in the future.

Measuring Tools

Whether or not you're trying to lose weight, consuming appropriate portion sizes is an essential part of a healthy, balanced diet. Our eyes often deceive us: Something as simple as the amount of meat or cheese layered on our sandwich can easily add up to extra calories we didn't even realize we were eating.

Measuring is also key for successful baking, which requires precision to properly execute a recipe. Unlike cooking, baking requires precision—

just the right balance of leavening and browning agents is needed.

To measure foods accurately, you need a few essential tools:

- A liquid measuring cup (2-cup capacity)

- A set of dry measuring cups (1-cup, ½-cup, ⅓-cup, and ¼-cup sizes)

- A set of measuring spoons (1 tablespoon, 1 teaspoon, ½ teaspoon, ¼ teaspoon)

- A food scale. The scale should measure pounds and ounces as well as grams. Most measurements will be in ounces, but for those foods concentrated in calories, portions are often measured in grams.

- A calculator

Cookware

Opt for nonstick cookware so you can heat foods without adding fat. Here are the basics you will need to have on hand:

- An ovenproof skillet or sauté pan with a lid

- A large (7-quart or bigger) stock or soup pot with a lid

- 1-quart and 3-quart saucepans with lids

- Several 15 × 10-inch baking sheets

- A roasting pan with a rack at the bottom

- A 9 × 13-inch casserole or baking dish

- A steamer (Some pots and pans come with a steamer insert; or you can buy a freestanding steamer basket that conforms to the pot you are using.)

CONVERSION TABLE FOR MEASURING PORTION SIZES

TEASPOONS	TABLESPOONS	CUPS	PINTS, QUARTS, GALLONS	FLUID OUNCES	MILLILITERS
1/4 teaspoon					1 ml
1/2 teaspoon					2 ml
1 teaspoon	1/3 tablespoon				5 ml
3 teaspoons	1 tablespoon	1/16 cup		1/2 oz	15 ml
6 teaspoons	2 tablespoons	1/8 cup		1 oz	30 ml
12 teaspoons	4 tablespoons	1/4 cup		2 oz	60 ml
16 teaspoons	5 1/3 tablespoons	1/3 cup		2 1/2 oz	75 ml
24 teaspoons	8 tablespoons	1/2 cup		4 oz	125 ml
32 teaspoons	10 2/3 tablespoons	2/3 cup		5 oz	150 ml
36 teaspoons	12 tablespoons	3/4 cup		6 oz	175 ml
48 teaspoons	16 tablespoons	1 cup	1/2 pint	8 oz	237 ml
		2 cups	1 pint	16 oz	473 ml
		3 cups		24 oz	710 ml
		4 cups	1 quart	32 oz	946 ml
		8 cups	1/2 gallon	64 oz	
		16 cups	1 gallon	128 oz	

- A colander
- Nonstick muffin pans, regular and miniature sizes

Cooking Utensils

The following implements are essential tools for any home cook and will make your time in the kitchen much more efficient:

- **Slotted spoon.** Helpful for lifting steamed, boiled, or poached items out of their cooking liquids.

- **Tongs.** Handy for grabbing meats off the grill and retrieving boiled vegetables, pasta, and other too-hot-to-handle items.

- **Spatulas.** A heatproof silicone spatula is perfect for lifting omelets, flipping pancakes, and more; a rubber baking spatula is helpful for hand-folding ingredients together and scraping the last bits of batter out of the bowl. Be sure to have a large metal spatula, as well, for turning burgers and other meats on the grill.

- **Whisk.** You'll need a metal whisk for mixing together dry ingredients or whipping egg whites in a metal bowl. It's also helpful to have a silicone whisk that won't damage nonstick pans.

- **Mixing spoon.** A wooden or silicone spoon, which won't transfer heat to your hand, is ideal for stirring sauces and soups.

- **Squeeze bottles.** These inexpensive containers allow you to aim, shoot, and squeeze small amounts of sauces in pretty designs on the plate. They can also help you dole out a portion that's just the right size.

- **Spray bottle.** Visit your local health food store for an oil spray bottle or mister, which will spritz a minimal amount of fat in the pan.

- **Handheld zester and grater.** This multitasking tool adds nutrition as well as flavor to your food. More than 50 percent of vitamin C in citrus fruits is in the peel, so add a dash of refreshing zest to your tea, salad, or hot cereal. Zesters are also handy for grating hard cheeses such as Parmesan—and by grating cheese finely, you can add a concentrated dusting of flavor without overdoing it on fat and calories.

- **Blender.** This versatile appliance is useful for making smoothies and creating a smooth, silky texture in blended soups and sauces.

- **Mini-chopper.** If you hate chopping garlic, a mini-chopper that holds just a cup or two is a lifesaver. Not essential, but definitely an affordable luxury.

- **Tenderizer.** This handheld tool resembles a mallet, made of wood or metal, flat on one side and with spikes or ridges on the other. Pummel your meat to break down tough fibers and give your marinades more places to seep in.

- **Mortar and pestle.** Another optional tool, but worth considering if you plan to buy and use whole spices. You can also use a clean electric coffee grinder to finely grind spices. I have two coffee grinders and use one for spices only.

- **Baking liners.** Use parchment paper when baking to avoid buttering or adding extra oil to pans or baking sheets, or you can try a reusable nonstick baking mat made of flexible silicone-based material. Parchment is also an eco-friendlier alternative to foil when wrapping foods to lock in moisture and flavor before baking in the oven.

THE FLAVOR FIRST PANTRY

Now that you're familiar with the techniques and tools that can add flavor to your foods, let's look at the pantry essentials that you can always rely on to dial up the flavor in any dish.

I've listed the herbs, spices, and other flavorings that I recommend you always have on hand in your pantry. If the list seems daunting, remember that it's best to buy in small quantities, as dried herbs and spices lose their potency in a year's time and many oils go rancid within an even shorter time frame (especially if you live in a warm climate).

Fresh Herbs

Unless you grow them yourself, you may want to buy fresh herbs as needed, because they don't typically keep in the refrigerator for more than a week and can be expensive to purchase. But it is nice to keep a few sprigs of your favorites on hand—nothing beats the flavor of tomatoes topped with freshly chopped basil or the herbaceous kick of parsley that's been added to meat or whole grains.

To preserve fresh herbs as long as possible, wash them immediately, drain or spin using a salad spinner, separate the stalks and snip off the bottoms of the stems. Then either place them in a jar of water in the fridge like a flower bouquet or wrap them in a just-damp paper towel and seal them in a plastic bag.

I recommend buying the following herbs fresh whenever possible:

- Basil
- Chives
- Cilantro
- Dill
- Flat-leaf (Italian) parsley
- Garlic
- Ginger
- Mint
- Oregano
- Tarragon
- Thyme

Dried Herbs

When herbs from the preceding list aren't readily available fresh, keep their dried counterparts on hand. I also recommend investing in the following dried herbs. As a rule of thumb, 1 tablespoon of fresh herbs equals about 1 teaspoon of dried.

- Bay leaves
- Marjoram
- Rosemary
- Sage

Spices

Whether you buy whole or ground spices, choose the smallest quantities you can to ensure freshness. If you want to experiment, check out the bulk food bins of your neighborhood health food store, which often stocks spices. You can buy just a couple of tablespoons at a time, allowing you to sample a wide variety of flavors at a minimal cost. I keep my spice rack stocked with the following flavorful spices:

- Allspice
- Aniseed
- Black pepper
- Cardamom
- Celery seed
- Chili powder
- Cinnamon
- Cloves
- Cumin
- Curry powder
- Fennel seed
- Ground ginger
- Ground mustard
- Mustard seed
- Paprika

- Poppy seed
- Red chile flakes
- Spice blends (look for low-sodium options for ready-mixed seasonings and spices)
- Turmeric

Other Flavorings

- Lavender
- Unsweetened cocoa powder
- Vanilla

Oils

Use canola or olive oil as your everyday cooking oil, and then add a dash of the more exotic and pricey oils for added flavor.

- Canola oil
- Extra-virgin or virgin olive oil
- Flaxseed oil
- Sesame oil
- Walnut oil

Vinegars

Experiment with these varieties to add flavor to everything from salad dressing to stew:

- Apple cider vinegar
- Balsamic vinegar
- Unseasoned rice wine vinegar

Sauces, Spreads, and Other Condiments

Always look for lower-salt versions of these zesty additions to your pantry. And if you buy condiments rather than make them, choose no-sugar-added varieties.

- Barbecue sauce and ketchup (no sugar added)
- Capers
- Dijon and brown mustards
- Fish sauce
- Fresh salsa
- Fruit spreads (no sugar added)
- Guacamole (fresh, no sour cream added)
- Horseradish
- *Pico de gallo*
- Soy sauce
- Tabasco sauce
- Tamari
- Worcestershire sauce

BREAKFAST

On a typical weekday morning, a leisurely meal is probably out of the question. Between packing school lunches, trying to squeeze in an early workout, and getting ready for work, who has time to cook?

But being on the go is no excuse for skipping the most important meal of the day. Eating a nutritious morning meal can put you on the path to smart food choices throughout the day. Consider these breakfast facts:

Eating breakfast lowers stress hormones. Cortisol, the hormone that makes us crave sweet, starchy foods, also makes our cells more insulin resistant, putting us at higher risk of diabetes. In addition, cortisol directs your body to store fat around your waistline, another risk factor for not only diabetes but also heart disease. Studies have shown that eating breakfast can lower levels of cortisol. So, by eating a morning meal, you'll not only feel satisfied and avoid hunger later in the day but also lower your risk of developing these life-threatening diseases.

Skipping meals wreaks havoc on blood sugar levels. The National Institute on Aging found that people who fasted during the day and consumed all their calories at one nightly meal exhibited unhealthy changes in their metabolisms, similar to unhealthy blood sugar levels observed in people with diabetes. The non-meal-skippers, on the other hand, consumed the same number of calories each day, but the calories were distributed throughout the day at three regular meal intervals; their blood sugar levels remained healthy. It may seem counterintuitive, but skipping meals promotes weight *gain,* not loss.

It's not just the act of eating breakfast that's important—*what* you eat is just as critical. The typical American breakfast skews heavily toward complex carbohydrates and refined foods such as pancakes, cereal, bagels, muffins, and doughnuts. But these foods are not only high in calories; their high sugar content can also cause an upswing in your blood sugar level. And after it peaks, it drops—making you feel sluggish and hungry (and craving a sweet pick-me-up).

Make breakfast an opportunity to start your day off right. Breakfast is not dessert!

Put protein front and center. Lean protein is not only essential for a balanced diet, it also helps balance the rise in blood sugar that can occur from eating carbohydrates, and makes you feel full longer than carbs alone. And because protein helps support muscle growth and maintenance, not eating enough can contribute to feelings of tiredness and muscle fatigue. You have a number of options for healthy protein at breakfast, such as lean breakfast meats (like the Italian Sausage Links on page 49), Greek yogurt, and of course, the breakfast standby: eggs.

Eggs are the centerpiece for many breakfast

dishes, from quiches to frittatas to plain old sunny side up or scrambled. And these days, you have more options than ever when it comes to this once-humble ingredient. So how do you know which eggs are the right choice for you? Here's a quick rundown on the egg-sentials:

- There are no fewer than six size grades for eggs, as determined by the USDA. Opt for "large" (2 to 2¼ ounces) eggs rather than "medium" (1¾ to 2 ounces) or "jumbo," unless a recipe indicates otherwise.

- Look for AA grade, the highest, for poaching, as the whites and yolks are most likely to remain intact; AA eggs are also easier to separate when you want to use just the whites. Grade A eggs suffice for baking.

- Egg substitute, sold in cartons, contains egg whites, milk, starches, and oil, and can be used in baking and cooking. Egg substitute is cholesterol free, but because of the additives it is an inferior alternative to the real thing.

- Omega-3 eggs are laid by chickens fed a diet high in omega-3 fatty acids. If you're not watching your cholesterol, they're a good option for increasing your intake of omega-3s. But if you don't eat yolks, don't bother paying extra for these nutritionally enhanced eggs, since the omega-3s are contained in the yolks only.

Choose the right grains. The bran and fiber in whole grains make it more difficult for digestive enzymes to break down the starches into glucose—leading to a slower, more moderate increase in blood sugar levels. Whole wheat breads, muffins, and cereals can all be part of a healthy breakfast that won't let you down later in the day.

When it comes to cereal, you have two choices: cold or hot. Both can be very satisfying in the morning, and both offer a host of nutritional benefits. Just be sure to shop carefully and choose whole grain items. When purchasing boxed cold cereals, read the labels and look for brands that contain more than 5 grams of fiber per serving, and less than 5 grams of sugar per serving.

Hot cereal options include more than just oatmeal. In fact, there are a variety of whole grain hot cereals available to you. Try one of these delicious grains in the morning:

- **Oatmeal** is the staple we know best. Most common are rolled or old-fashioned oats, which take about 15 minutes to cook. Steel-cut or Scotch oats are chopped with a steel blade; they take longer to cook and have a decidedly chewy texture. Steer clear of instant oatmeal packets;

they're usually packed with added sugar and contain far less fiber.

- **Grits** are made from ground hominy (hulled white or yellow corn kernels) and have a slightly sweet taste, similar to corn on the cob. Grits can be prepared like oatmeal and are delicious with fruit.

- **Polenta** is coarsely ground cornmeal. Often served as a savory accompaniment to meat at dinner, polenta can also be enjoyed at breakfast or sweetened as a dessert.

- **Porridge** refers to any combination of grains cooked to a thick, puddinglike consistency. Oatmeal is the most common ingredient, but porridge can also include barley, groats, or bulgur.

The recipes that follow offer a variety of options for balanced breakfasts, from savory to sweet. Each of these dishes offers healthy nutrition and plenty of flavor to start out your day on a delicious note.

GO NORTH OF THE BORDER FOR BACON

Taken from the lean, tender eye of the loin in the pig's back, Canadian bacon is actually closer kin to ham than to regular bacon, which comes from the side of the pig. Canadian bacon is sold precooked, so it shrinks less in preparation and therefore provides more servings per pound. Canadian bacon also has 35 percent less sodium, 65 percent fewer calories, and 75 percent less fat than traditional bacon.

This satisfying, high-protein breakfast can be prepared the night before. In the morning, just pop the quichettes in the microwave or eat them cold—they're delicious either way. Store extras in small plastic bags for quick grab 'n' go snacks.

SPINACH AND HAM QUICHETTES

MAKES 6 (3-QUICHETTE) SERVINGS

1 (10-ounce) package frozen spinach (see note), thawed and squeezed dry

3 large eggs, preferably omega-3 enriched

2 large egg whites

1 (15-ounce) container fat-free ricotta cheese

1 teaspoon minced garlic

½ teaspoon ground mustard

1 teaspoon canola oil

4 (½-ounce) slices Canadian bacon, diced

½ cup diced onion

1 cup (4 ounces) shredded low-fat Cheddar cheese

1 tablespoon grated Parmesan cheese

Preheat the oven to 425°F with an oven rack in the upper third. Lightly coat 18 muffin cups with cooking spray.

Combine the spinach, whole eggs, egg whites, ricotta, garlic, and mustard in a food processor. Process just until combined. Pour into a large bowl and set aside.

In a nonstick skillet, heat the oil. Add the bacon and onion and cook for 3 minutes, or until the onion is soft. Let cool slightly. Add to the egg mixture along with the Cheddar and Parmesan and stir to combine. There will be about 6 cups.

Pour about ⅓ cup of the mixture into each of the prepared muffin cups. Bake for 15 minutes, or until just set.

Note: The frozen spinach can be replaced with an equal weight of fresh, wilted spinach. To wilt, cook the spinach with 1 tablespoon or less of water in a 12-inch nonstick skillet for 3 to 5 minutes, or until the leaves wilt and become soft. Cool, blot excess water using paper towels, and use as directed in the recipe.

Per serving: 190 calories, 6 g total fat (2 g saturated), 125 mg cholesterol, 350 mg sodium, 10 g total carbohydrates (4 g sugars), 2 g fiber, 21 g protein

Toast your oats! Substituting toasted oats in your favorite oat recipes imparts a nutty, rich flavor to your dish. To toast oats (or in this case, oat flour), spread them out on a baking sheet and bake at 350°F for about 10 minutes, stirring halfway. The resulting flavor is well worth the extra time and effort.

TOASTED OATCAKES WITH BERRY CONFETTI

MAKES 14 (4-INCH) OR 28 (2-INCH) OATCAKES

1	cup stone-ground polenta
¾	cup oat flour (see note)
¼	cup untoasted wheat germ
2	tablespoons ground flaxseed
2	teaspoons baking powder
¼	teaspoon salt
1	large egg
1	egg white
¼	cup canola, grapeseed, or light olive oil
1¾–2	cups low-fat buttermilk
½	cup chopped dried fruit (any combination of cranberries, blueberries, cherries, currants, and raisins)
	Maple syrup (optional; see note)

Combine the polenta, oat flour, wheat germ, flaxseed, baking powder, and salt in a medium bowl.

Whisk together the whole egg, egg white, oil, and 1¾ cups of the buttermilk in another bowl. Add the buttermilk mixture to the flour mixture all at once and whisk just until combined. Fold in the dried fruit. There will be about 3½ cups of batter. Allow the batter to stand for about 20 minutes or refrigerate overnight. If the batter is too thick (it should be the consistency of thick cream), add as much as ¼ cup more buttermilk.

Preheat a nonstick griddle. Lightly coat with cooking spray. Ladle or spoon the batter onto the preheated pan, using ¼ cup of batter to make 4-inch oatcakes or 2 tablespoons for 2-inch oatcakes. Turn the oatcakes when the tops bubble and the outer edges begin to firm up. Serve immediately. Top with syrup if desired.

Note: To make your own oat flour, blend old-fashioned rolled oats in a blender or food processor.

Note: Two tablespoons of pure maple syrup per serving will add 80 calories.

Per serving (one 4-inch or two 2-inch oatcakes): 120 calories, 6 g total fat (<1 g saturated), 15 mg cholesterol, 125 mg sodium, 15 g total carbohydrates (2 g sugars), 2 g fiber, 3 g protein

Traditionally served with sherry for dessert, this nutritious, teetotaling version of the classic ambrosia salad makes for a scrumptious, protein-packed breakfast or snack. The quality and freshness of the fruit will impact the taste of the entire dish, so be sure to use the best fruit you can find. Feel free to swap in your favorite fruits, if you prefer—fruits vary in size, but you want to aim for about 4 cups total.

AMBROSIA WITH VANILLA YOGURT CREAM

MAKES 6 (¾-CUP) SERVINGS

YOGURT CREAM

- 1½ cups fat-free plain Greek yogurt
- 1 teaspoon vanilla extract
- 1 packet stevia or 1 tablespoon honey or agave nectar

FRUIT AND GARNISH

- 1 medium banana, diced
- 2 medium kiwifruit, peeled and diced
- 1 cup sliced strawberries
- ½ cup halved red grapes
- ¼ cup chopped pecans, toasted
- ¼ cup unsweetened shredded coconut, toasted (see note)

  Fresh mint leaves (optional)

To make the yogurt cream: Combine the yogurt, vanilla extract, and sweetener in a small bowl.

To assemble the fruit and garnish: Gently toss the banana, kiwi, strawberries, and grapes in a large bowl. Divide among 6 parfait glasses or small bowls. Top with the yogurt cream. Sprinkle the nuts and coconut on top just before serving. Garnish with fresh mint, if desired.

Note: Coconut can be toasted in the oven or on the stove top. For oven toasting, spread the coconut in an even layer on a rimmed baking sheet. Bake at 325°F for 15 to 20 minutes, stirring every 5 minutes for even browning. For stove-top toasting, spread the coconut in a small skillet and toast over medium heat, stirring often, until the coconut is light golden brown.

Per serving: 140 calories, 6 g total fat (2 g saturated), 0 mg cholesterol, 20 mg sodium, 16 g total carbohydrates (11 g sugars), 3 g fiber, 6 g protein

This delicious, high-protein, gluten-free grain is not just for savory dishes. Quinoa is extremely versatile and can be used in a variety of dishes, from breakfast to dessert. For a sweeter breakfast bowl, add 1 to 2 tablespoons agave nectar or honey.

APPLE-CINNAMON BREAKFAST QUINOA

MAKES 4 (¾-CUP) SERVINGS

2 cups unsweetened plain or vanilla almond milk (see Shopping Sources/ Nondairy Milk, page 203)

1 cup dry quinoa, well rinsed (see note)

1 medium apple, diced

1 teaspoon ground cinnamon

Pinch of salt

½ teaspoon vanilla extract

GARNISH (OPTIONAL)

¼ cup dried currants

¼ cup chopped toasted almonds or walnuts

Fresh mint leaves, sliced

In a 2-quart saucepan, heat the almond milk over medium-high heat. When the milk is almost boiling, stir in the quinoa, apple, cinnamon, and salt. Reduce the heat, partially cover, and simmer for about 15 minutes, or until most of the milk has been absorbed. Remove from the heat. Stir in the vanilla extract, cover tightly, and let rest for 5 minutes. Fluff with a fork before serving. Garnish with currants, nuts, and mint, if desired.

Note: After measuring, rinse quinoa with cold water in a fine strainer to ensure that any saponins are removed. These plant chemicals can add a bitter taste to your cooked quinoa if not thoroughly rinsed away.

Per serving: 200 calories, 4 g total fat (0 g saturated), 0 mg cholesterol, 95 mg sodium, 35 g total carbohydrates (5 g sugars), 5 g fiber, 7 g protein

The whole family will love this flavorful, protein-packed breakfast—it's sure to become a weekend favorite in your household. You might want to have a little extra sofrito sauce on hand for those who enjoy their eggs with an extra kick of heat.

HUEVOS SOFRITO

MAKES 4 SERVINGS

4   (1-ounce) slices Canadian bacon

4   corn tortillas (6-inch diameter)

8   egg whites or 4 large eggs

1   cup Easy Sofrito Sauce (page 176), heated, plus more to taste

¼   cup shredded low-fat pepper Jack cheese

2   tablespoons chopped cilantro, for garnish

In a small nonstick skillet, warm the Canadian bacon over medium heat until just warmed through. Transfer the bacon to a plate and cover to keep warm. In the same skillet, warm each tortilla over medium heat for about 30 seconds per side. Cover to keep warm.

Coat a nonstick skillet with cooking spray. Add the egg whites or whole eggs and cook, without stirring, for 2 minutes, or until nearly set. Turn the eggs with a silicone spatula and finish cooking, about 1 minute longer.

To serve, place a warm tortilla on a plate and top with 1 slice of Canadian bacon. Place 2 egg whites or a single egg on top of the bacon. Top the egg(s) with ¼ cup hot sofrito sauce and sprinkle with 1 tablespoon cheese. Garnish with the cilantro.

Per serving: 170 calories, 5 g total fat (2 g saturated), 25 mg cholesterol, 420 mg sodium, 14 g total carbohydrates (2 g sugars), 2 g fiber, 18 g protein

This impressive-looking dish is perfect for an elegant brunch or breakfast when you have overnight guests. It tastes and looks indulgent but contains just 200 calories per serving.

SCRAMBLED EGGS WITH PROSCIUTTO AND ROASTED ASPARAGUS

MAKES 2 SERVINGS

½ pound trimmed asparagus, cut on the diagonal into 1-inch pieces (about 1¼ cups)

2 teaspoons canola or olive oil

Salt and ground black pepper to taste (optional)

1 large egg

5 large egg whites

2 tablespoons 1% milk

½ teaspoon Italian herb blend

1 ounce prosciutto (about 4 thin slices) or Canadian bacon (about 1 slice), diced

1 teaspoon grated Parmesan cheese

2 sprigs fresh thyme, leaves removed from stems

Place the asparagus on a baking sheet and drizzle with 1 teaspoon of the oil. Season with salt and pepper, if desired, and toss to coat. Distribute the spears in a single layer on the pan. Roast for 5 to 8 minutes, or until tender but still crisp. Remove from the oven and set aside.

While the asparagus is roasting, whisk the whole egg, egg whites, milk, and herb blend in a bowl. In a medium nonstick skillet, heat the remaining 1 teaspoon oil. Pour the egg mixture into the skillet and cook over low heat, stirring constantly with a wooden spoon. Cook the eggs for about 3 minutes, or until they are no longer runny but still soft. Remove the skillet from the heat, add the roasted asparagus and prosciutto or Canadian bacon, and stir to combine. Spoon the mixture onto plates and garnish each serving with a sprinkle of Parmesan and thyme leaves.

Per serving: 200 calories, 10 g total fat (2 g saturated), 115 mg cholesterol, 420 mg sodium, 9 g total carbohydrates (5 g sugars), 3 g fiber, 21 g protein

It's getting easier to find high-fiber, whole grain baked goods, but nothing beats the taste (or smell) of freshly baked bread. Though this recipe uses two packages of yeast, the bread is still very dense—and absolutely delicious when toasted. If you can't find flaxseed meal, you can purchase whole flaxseeds and grind them in a clean coffee grinder.

WHOLE GRAIN APPLE-CINNAMON BREAD

MAKES 1 (2-POUND) LOAF, OR 16 SLICES

1 cup unsweetened apple juice

¾ cup water

1 tablespoon canola or olive oil

1 tablespoon honey or agave nectar

2 packages active dry yeast (see note on page 48)

3 cups white whole wheat flour (I used King Arthur brand)

¾ cup wheat or oat bran

¾ cup diced prunes, dried currants, or raisins

½ cup chopped toasted walnuts (optional)

¼ cup ground flaxseed

2 tablespoons + 1 teaspoon vital wheat gluten (see note on page 48)

1 tablespoon ground cinnamon

2 teaspoons salt

1 teaspoon vanilla extract

Heat the apple juice and water to 110° to 115°F in the microwave, checking with a thermometer. Combine the juice mixture, oil, honey or agave nectar, and yeast in a large bowl. Allow the mixture to rest for 5 minutes to activate the yeast (see note).

Combine the flour, bran, fruit, flaxseed, wheat gluten, cinnamon, salt, and vanilla extract in a separate bowl. Make a well in the flour mixture and pour in the yeast mixture. Use your hands to mix the dough together and turn out onto a lightly floured board. Knead for 5 minutes, form the dough into a ball, and place in a lightly oiled bowl. Cover the bowl with plastic wrap or a kitchen towel and let rise until doubled, about 2 hours.

Uncover the bowl and punch the dough down.

Turn the dough out onto a lightly floured surface and knead gently for a minute or two. Shape into a loaf and place in a lightly oiled 8 × 4-inch loaf pan. Cover and let rise until doubled, 1½ to 2 hours.

Meanwhile, preheat the oven to 400°F.

Make 4 slashes across the top of the dough with cuts up to ¼ inch deep. Bake for 45 minutes, or until the crust is golden brown.

(continued)

Remove the bread from the oven and spray lightly with cooking spray. Cool, in the pan, to room temperature before slicing or storing.

Note: Be sure to check the expiration date on your yeast package and read the directions carefully. If the yeast doesn't bubble or activate, it is probably expired, or the water and juice mixture wasn't the right temperature. A bubbly mixture is a sign that the yeast is activated and will make your bread dough rise. If your yeast mixture doesn't bubble, throw it out and start over.

Note: Vital wheat gluten is a protein-rich food related to seitan, which is sometimes called "wheat meat." Seitan is a solid that's packaged in small cakes like tofu or in tubs like yogurt; vital wheat gluten is the same substance in powdered form. Vital wheat gluten is available in health food stores; look for brands such as Arrowhead Mills and Bob's Red Mill. For additional information on finding vital wheat gluten, see Shopping Sources on page 200.

Per slice: 150 calories, 2 g total fat (0 g saturated), 0 mg cholesterol, 300 mg sodium, 29 g total carbohydrates (5 g sugars), 6 g fiber, 5 g protein

FLAX: A LITTLE SEED WITH BIG HEALTH BENEFITS

Flaxseed is a preeminent plant source of alpha-linolenic acid, or ALA, which our bodies convert into essential omega-3 fatty acids. Omega-3s offer anti-aging benefits, help regulate beneficial hormone production, and protect heart function by reducing blood clotting and preventing irregular heartbeat. Omega-3s are also thought to reduce arthritis symptoms and the onset of Alzheimer's disease.

You may not think of pork as a lean protein, but tenderloin is a healthy and flavorful cut of pork. These sausages make a hearty breakfast and can also be grilled and sliced for a quick appetizer, or cooked and crumbled for a pizza topping. They contain half the calories of most lean turkey Italian sausages and a lot less sodium.

ITALIAN SAUSAGE LINKS

MAKES 8 (4-INCH) LINKS

1	pound pork tenderloin (or very lean ground pork)
2	teaspoons minced garlic
½	teaspoon fennel seed
½	teaspoon onion powder
½	teaspoon salt
¼	teaspoon dried basil
¼	teaspoon dried oregano
¼	teaspoon ground black pepper
¼	teaspoon red chile flakes (optional)
2	teaspoons canola oil

Remove all visible fat from the pork. Cut the pork into ½-inch pieces.

Combine the pork, garlic, fennel seed, onion powder, salt, basil, oregano, black pepper, and chile flakes, if desired, in a food processor. Pulse just until the mixture is well combined and cohesive (but not pureed). Transfer to a bowl, cover with plastic, and refrigerate for at least 1 hour (or overnight) to allow the flavors to combine. There will be about 2 cups of mixture.

Using approximately ¼ cup of the mixture per sausage, quickly shape into 8 links about 1 inch in diameter and 4 inches long.

In a large nonstick skillet, heat the oil over medium heat. Add the sausages, cover, and cook for 3 minutes. Turn the sausages, reduce the heat to medium-low, cover, and cook for about 2 minutes longer, or until crisp and cooked through. Be sure to monitor closely for doneness, as overcooked sausages will be dry.

When the sausages are cooked through, remove from the pan and drain on paper towels. Serve hot.

Per link: 80 calories, 3 g total fat (1 g saturated), 40 mg cholesterol, 170 mg sodium, 1 g total carbohydrates (0 g sugars), 0 g fiber, 12 g protein

APPETIZERS AND SNACKS

Eating less may seem like a smart strategy when you're trying to lose weight. But in fact, there are benefits to eating more—more *often,* that is.

Eating small snacks throughout the day prevents you from becoming famished at any point. And as we all know, it's when we're "starving" that we're the most likely to reach for unhealthy foods and overeat. Even if you're not watching your weight, there are benefits to eating several small meals throughout the day as opposed to two or three large meals. Eating regular, small portions keeps your blood sugar stable and helps your body recognize (and listen to) hunger and satiety cues—the signals that let us know when we need to eat and when to stop.

Of course, no matter how often you eat, the trick is to choose wisely, whether it's your midmorning coffee break or a midafternoon pick-me-up. Many foods packaged for convenience and marketed specifically for snacking are anything but healthy: chips, cookies, and even snack-size yogurts can be loaded with sugar and empty calories. And many of those "100-calorie snack packs" are simply smaller portions of junk foods, that offer little in the way of nutrition.

Sampling a few nibbles of a variety of dishes is also an easy, fun way to satisfy your craving for various flavors and textures when you're celebrating or entertaining. By making your own healthy, delicious snacks and party foods, you'll get all the satisfaction that comes with snacking without any of the guilt. The recipes in this chapter can be served as appetizers, snacks, or first courses, or even paired with one another to create a variety of small plates for a main course. These simple, no-fuss dishes are real crowd-pleasers. And at 150 calories or less per serving, you can feel free to snack till you're satisfied!

Here are a few tips for creating lower-calorie versions of your favorite indulgences:

Ditch the chips. Serve dips and spreads with a pretty arrangement of seasonal vegetables, such as radishes, multicolored "dwarf" carrots, summer squash, and thin-sliced "chips" made from jicama—a crispy, slightly sweet, edible root that can be eaten raw. If you have a craving only chips will satisfy, opt for baked varieties, or create your own baked chips in the oven from whole grain tortillas and pita bread.

Create richness without fat. The creamy texture is often what we crave in a dip—but most recipes achieve it with an overdose of fat in the form of sour cream, cream cheese, or heavy cream. Try swapping in fat-free or low-fat versions of these dairy products or use fat-free Greek yogurt as a substitute. You'll achieve a creamy texture with a lot less fat and calories. You can also create a creamy dip or spread without dairy, if you choose. Try using avocado in place of mayo, and adding miso paste to dips for a richer mouthfeel.

Skip frying, keep the crunch. As we all know, deep-fried foods are a dietary disaster. Fried foods are not only high in calories, but the rapid oxidation of oil in extreme heat creates carcinogenic compounds and trans fats that contribute to hardened arteries, elevated cholesterol, and heart disease. Instead of frying to achieve a crisp texture, try spraying your food with a light mist of canola or olive oil before baking to crispy perfection.

GO GREEK

Greek yogurt is strained more than other yogurts—a process that removes most of the watery whey and gives the yogurt a rich, creamy texture. Since whey is mostly carbohydrate, the strained yogurt contains less carbohydrate and is more concentrated in protein. One cup of fat-free plain Greek yogurt has approximately 100 calories, 5 grams of carbohydrate, and a whopping 20 grams of protein—more than double the amount per serving in most regular yogurts.

Though this recipe is perfectly scrumptious served as a classic shrimp cocktail made with steamed shrimp, grilling shrimp adds a rich layer of smoky flavor to this timeless appetizer.

GRILLED SHRIMP WITH FIRE-ROASTED COCKTAIL SAUCE

MAKES 4 SERVINGS

1 tablespoon olive oil

½ teaspoon Garlic Salt (page 193)

16 jumbo shrimp (about 1 pound), peeled and deveined

1 cup Fire-Roasted Cocktail Sauce (page 175)

1 tablespoon chopped flat-leaf (Italian) parsley

1 lemon, cut into 4 wedges or 8 slices

Preheat a grill to medium-high or preheat a grill pan over medium-high heat.

Combine the oil and Garlic Salt in a medium bowl. Add the shrimp and toss well.

If using a grill, place the shrimp on skewers before placing on the grill. Place the shrimp on the grill or grill pan and cook for about 3 minutes on each side, or until pink and firm. Remove from the heat.

Spoon ¼ cup of cocktail sauce into each of 4 decorative glasses. Top with 4 shrimp per glass. Sprinkle with the parsley and garnish with the lemon wedges or slices.

Per serving: 150 calories, 5 g total fat (1 g saturated), 170 mg cholesterol, 340 mg sodium, 2 g total carbohydrates (1 g sugars), 0 g fiber, 23 g protein

Once the sofrito sauce is made, these tacos take just minutes to prepare. If you don't like cheese (who doesn't?), you can double the amount of avocado instead. If you don't have avocado on hand, double the cheese! And if you don't eat meat—substitute roasted mushrooms.

BAKED TACOS

MAKES 8 SERVINGS

- 8 corn tortillas (6-inch diameter)
- 1 cup Easy Sofrito Sauce (page 176) or pureed tomato salsa
- 2 cups cooked, crumbled lean ground beef, chicken, or turkey
- ½ cup (2 ounces) shredded reduced-fat Mexican 4-cheese blend

  Red chile flakes to taste (optional)
- ½ firm-ripe Hass avocado, finely diced (about ½ cup)

Preheat the oven to 475°F.

Place the tortillas on a nonstick baking sheet. Spread each tortilla with 2 tablespoons of the sofrito sauce, leaving a ½-inch border around the edges. Sprinkle each taco with ¼ cup of the crumbled meat and 1 tablespoon of the cheese. Sprinkle with chile flakes, if desired.

Bake for 6 to 7 minutes, or until the cheese melts and the edges just start to brown. Remove from the oven. Loosen from the pan. Sprinkle each with 1 tablespoon diced avocado and fold in half, pressing the edges of the tortilla lightly together. Serve immediately.

Per serving: 150 calories, 4 g total fat (1 g saturated), 20 mg cholesterol, 160 mg sodium, 15 g total carbohydrates (2 g sugars), 3 g fiber, 14 g protein

I love the flavor of smoked trout, but if you prefer, you can use smoked salmon or canned pink salmon in this addictive dip. Serve it as an elegant appetizer with whole grain crackers or spread on whole grain bagels for a breakfast treat.

SMOKY TROUT SPREAD

MAKES 8 (¼-CUP) SERVINGS

1 cup fat-free plain Greek yogurt

4 ounces Neufchâtel cream cheese

½ medium red bell pepper, roasted and peeled (see note)

1 tablespoon + 1 teaspoon horseradish

2 teaspoons lime juice

1 teaspoon Dijon mustard

4 ounces smoked trout (see note), finely chopped

2 tablespoons chopped shallots

1 tablespoon chopped fresh chives

Combine the yogurt, cream cheese, roasted pepper, horseradish, lime juice, and mustard in a food processor and combine until smooth. Transfer to a bowl and stir in the trout and shallots. Refrigerate for at least 1 hour. Transfer to a serving dish and garnish with the chives.

Note: If substituting salmon, use an equal amount of smoked salmon or 4 ounces drained canned wild salmon.

Note: Roast the whole bell pepper under a broiler or over a gas flame, turning occasionally, until the skin blisters and chars all over. Place in a bowl, cover with a lid, and allow to steam to loosen the skin, or place in a paper bag. Carefully peel away the skin and remove the seeds.

Per serving: 80 calories, 3 g total fat (2 g saturated), 20 mg cholesterol, 65 mg sodium, 3 g total carbohydrates (1 g sugars), 0 g fiber, 8 g protein

Caramelizing is one of my favorite ways to add layers of rich flavor to the simplest of ingredients, in this case, plain yellow onions. It takes a little bit of time for the onions to caramelize, but the end result is worth it. This dip is positively addictive when served with a colorful platter of crudités.

CHUNKY ONION DIP

MAKES 12 (¼-CUP) SERVINGS

2½   pounds yellow onions, peeled

1   tablespoon olive oil

1   teaspoon salt

1   tablespoon onion powder

4   ounces Neufchâtel cream cheese, room temperature

¾   cup fat-free plain Greek yogurt

Flat-leaf (Italian) parsley leaves, for garnish (optional)

Halve the onions lengthwise and then slice them crosswise into ⅛-inch-thick half-rounds. There will be about 4 cups.

In a large skillet, heat the oil over medium heat. Add the onions and salt and cook for 2 to 3 minutes. Reduce the heat to low, cover, and cook, stirring occasionally, for 15 minutes, or until the onions are soft and beginning to release their juices. Continue to simmer uncovered, stirring occasionally, for 15 to 20 minutes longer, or until the onions are lightly browned and caramelized. Allow to cool. There will be about 2 cups.

Place the onions in a food processor and pulse a few times to chop. Remove half of the onions and transfer them to a bowl. To the remaining onions in the food processor, add the onion powder and process until pureed. Add the cream cheese and yogurt and process just until smooth. Transfer the mixture to the bowl and fold into the chopped onions.

Taste and season as needed. Chill for at least 1 hour. Transfer the dip to a serving bowl and garnish with parsley leaves, if desired.

Per serving: 80 calories, 3 g total fat (1 g saturated), 5 mg cholesterol, 230 mg sodium, 11 g total carbohydrates (5 g sugars), 1 g fiber, 3 g protein

This Middle Eastern eggplant dip is traditionally served with warm pita bread and an assortment of salads. Be sure to use whole wheat pita bread, or substitute fresh crudités for dipping. This is a great make-ahead dish and keeps in the refrigerator for several days.

BABA GHANOUJ

MAKES 16 (¼-CUP) SERVINGS

2 large eggplants (about 1½ pounds each)

1 cup fat-free plain Greek yogurt

½ cup tahini (see note)

⅓ cup lemon juice

1 tablespoon ground cumin

1 tablespoon minced garlic

2 teaspoons white wine vinegar

2 teaspoons salt (optional)

¼ cup finely chopped flat-leaf (Italian) parsley leaves

Note: A Middle Eastern specialty, tahini is a thick paste made from ground sesame seeds. It's increasingly available in supermarkets.

Wash and dry the eggplants. Cut off the stem ends. Pierce the skin with a fork several times.

To grill: Grill the eggplants either on an outdoor grill or indoors over a gas burner. Place the eggplants directly on the grill rack or over two gas burners at medium heat. Grill for about 18 minutes, turning frequently to cook evenly, or until very soft.

To roast: Preheat the oven to 350°F with an oven rack in the center position. Lightly coat a 15 × 10-inch baking sheet with olive oil cooking spray. Place the eggplants on the baking sheet and bake for about 40 minutes, turning the eggplants three or four times to roast evenly, until very soft. Set aside to cool. When cool enough to handle, peel and discard the skin. Discard most of the seeds and cut the eggplants into chunks.

Combine the yogurt, tahini, lemon juice, cumin, garlic, and vinegar in a food processor and puree until smooth. If the mixture is very thick, add hot water by tablespoons to achieve the right consistency. Add the eggplant chunks and pulse just to combine. The mixture will be a bit chunky. Taste and adjust the seasoning with salt if necessary. Garnish with the parsley.

Per serving: 69 calories, 4 g total fat (<1 g saturated), 0 mg cholesterol, 15 mg sodium, 3 g total carbohydrates (2 g sugars), 3 g fiber, 3 g protein

Roasting tomatillos adds a rich dimension to one of our favorite (and ridiculously low-calorie) condiments. Salsa can be used to spice up just about any dish, from eggs to grilled fish. And of course, it's a great snack with baked whole grain chips. Stir in a few tablespoons of diced avocado for added richness and flavor.

ROASTED TOMATILLO SALSA

MAKES 12 (1/4-CUP) SERVINGS

1 pound tomatillos, husks removed, rinsed

1 cup canned no-salt-added fire-roasted diced tomatoes

1 red bell pepper, roasted (see note, page 57), peeled, and coarsely chopped

1/2 cup coarsely chopped cilantro

1 tablespoon lime juice

2 teaspoons chopped garlic

1 teaspoon Chipotle Puree (optional; page 192)

Salt

Preheat the broiler or the grill. Broil or grill the tomatillos until their skins blister and just begin to char, about 5 minutes. Set aside to cool for about 10 minutes.

Combine the tomatillos, tomatoes, roasted pepper, cilantro, lime juice, garlic, Chipotle Puree (if desired), and 1/2 teaspoon of salt in a food processor. Pulse until the ingredients are finely chopped but not pureed. Season to taste with additional salt.

Per serving: 20 calories, 0 g total fat (0 g saturated), 0 mg cholesterol, 150 mg sodium, 4 g total carbohydrates (3 g sugars), 1 g fiber, 1 g protein

THE MEXICAN TOMATO

Also called Mexican green tomatoes, tomatillos look like cherry tomatoes except that they are covered by a thin, papery husk. They can ripen to yellow but are generally picked and used while still green and firm. While fresh tomatillos tend to be sold seasonally in specialty markets, canned varieties are more widely available. Not only do they lend a lemony, herbaceous flavor to salsa and other foods, they also pack a powerful punch of vitamins A and C.

This flavorful appetizer was inspired by a dish I tasted at my friend Zov's eponymous restaurant in Tustin, California. If you can't find sumac locally, check the Shopping Sources under Herbs and Spices (page 202).

SPICY BEEF SATAYS

MAKES 8 (2-SKEWER) SERVINGS

1 pound flank steak, trimmed of any external fat

½ cup fat-free plain Greek yogurt

2 tablespoons lime juice

1 tablespoon smoked paprika

1 tablespoon ground sumac

1 teaspoon ground cumin

1 teaspoon Garlic Salt (page 193)

1 teaspoon ground mustard

¼ teaspoon ground allspice

3 tablespoons chopped cilantro

Lime wedges

Cut the flank steak across the grain into 16 strips.

Combine the yogurt, lime juice, smoked paprika, sumac, cumin, Garlic Salt, mustard, allspice, and 2 tablespoons of the cilantro in a medium bowl. Add the beef and stir well to coat completely. Cover tightly and refrigerate for at least 4 hours or overnight.

Remove the beef strips from the refrigerator and thread them on 16 skewers. Heat the grill to medium and place the skewers on the grill. Cook for about 2 minutes on each side for medium and about 3 minutes on each side for well-done.

Place the skewers on a serving dish. Garnish with lime wedges and the remaining 1 tablespoon cilantro.

Per serving: 90 calories, 3 g total fat (1 g saturated), 20 mg cholesterol, 200 mg sodium, 1 g total carbohydrates (0 g sugars), 0 g fiber, 14 g protein

SOUPS AND SALADS

Eating more soups and salads—not just as appetizers, but also as entrées—is an easy way to boost your intake of fruits and vegetables and slash your calorie consumption. Soups are often loaded with vegetables and intensely flavored with herbs and spices. And soup can satisfy your yen for almost any kind of texture, from rustic and chunky to silky smooth.

Salads have a reputation for being boring, but in fact, they are some of the most versatile dishes you can make. The combinations of fruits, vegetables, and proteins in salads are limited only by your imagination and what's in season at the market.

Both salads and soups can be prepared in large batches, making them easy "plan-ahead" meals. You can whip up a large salad on Sunday night and store it in small containers for quick lunches throughout the week (just be sure not to dress the salad until you plan to eat it). Or try cooking a big batch of soup on the weekend that can fill your freezer for many weeknight dinners to come. All you need to do at the end of a hectic day is defrost and dig in!

As with any dish, healthy preparation methods and ingredients are key to making these staples as nutritious as possible. For results that are rich with flavor but low in calories and fat:

Make friends with stock. Soup stock is a handy staple: You can use it to boil rice and other grains, moisten meats, and, of course, create a base for soup. By making stock at home, you can vary the flavorings and ingredients to suit your tastes. But if you don't have hours to simmer stock on the stove,

it's perfectly fine to go the store-bought route. Just be sure to study the labels carefully, as most canned stocks and bouillon cubes are high in sodium. Look for low-sodium, fat-free varieties.

Go easy on the dairy. You can impart a silky texture to soups by blending them and pressing them through a strainer, rather than adding cream or butter. And when composing a salad, add cheese as an accent to the vegetables, rather than the main ingredient. If you crave a creamy topping for your salad, use low-fat or fat-free Greek yogurt as a dressing base. Yogurt is also a good option when you want a creamy dollop in your soup.

Use meat, poultry, and fish as the garnish. Load your recipes with vegetables, and use legumes without hesitation—they're both filling and a good source of protein. Use animal proteins sparingly to enhance the flavors and provide contrasting textures, rather than as the centerpiece of the dish.

Make it a meal with whole grains. Adding barley or bulgur to a vegetable soup transforms an appetizer into a hearty one-course meal. And grain salads such as tabbouleh are a filling and refreshing alternative to higher-calorie, starchy salads such as macaroni or potato salad.

Create flavor by roasting. Roasting vegetables such as peppers, eggplant, and squash before pureeing into a soup adds a smoky, rich taste. Or combine flavors and textures in salads by mixing raw, crispy vegetables such as lettuce and cucumbers with soft, roasted peppers or onions.

ALL ABOUT ARTICHOKES

Artichokes have a meaty satisfying texture that makes a perfect addition to many soups and salads, such as the minestrone soup on page 71. The flower bud of a large plant from the thistle family, a whole artichoke has large, petal-shaped leaves. You can eat the cooked leaves by breaking them off one by one and using your teeth to scrape the tasty pulp from the base. Once the leaves are gone, the inedible choke of the flower is left—as is the flavorful, tender heart. When shopping for canned artichoke hearts, look for those that are packed in water rather than oil.

I used to pronounce this recipe differently each time I made it. My friends started calling it "Some Young Guy." Though it's traditionally made with whole coconut milk, I think it tastes just as fabulous made with light coconut milk.

TOM KA GAI (COCONUT CHICKEN SOUP)

MAKES 6 (1-CUP) SERVINGS

2 teaspoons canola oil

3 tablespoons minced fresh Thai ginger (galangal) or regular ginger

3 tablespoons chopped shallots

2 stalks fresh lemongrass (bottom 4 inches only), peeled, halved lengthwise, and thinly sliced crosswise

2½ cups fat-free, low-sodium chicken broth

1 (14-ounce) can light coconut milk

¼ cup Thai fish sauce (see note)

¼ cup lime juice

12 ounces boneless, skinless chicken breast, diced

1 cup thinly sliced mushrooms, preferably shiitakes

½ cup carrot matchsticks

2 tablespoons thinly sliced scallions

1 tablespoon chopped cilantro

In a 3-quart saucepan, heat the oil over medium-high heat. Add the ginger, shallots, and lemongrass and cook for about 1 minute, or until fragrant.

Carefully add the broth and coconut milk. Bring to a boil. Reduce the heat to a simmer, add the fish sauce and lime juice, and return to a simmer. Add the chicken, mushrooms, and carrots to the broth and cook for 3 minutes, or until the chicken is just cooked through.

Remove from the heat. Garnish with the scallions and cilantro and serve hot.

Note: Fish sauce, also called nuoc mam, is available in Asian markets, specialty foods stores, and some supermarkets.

Per serving: 170 calories, 5 g total fat (3 g saturated), 20 mg cholesterol, 980 mg sodium, 17 g total carbohydrates (3 g sugars), 2 g fiber, 11 g protein

THE MIRACLE ROOT

Ginger not only packs a flavor punch, it also offers a host of health benefits. Ginger is high in disease-fighting antioxidants and helps the liver and gallbladder break down fats and rid your body of toxins. Ginger is even considered to be a homeopathic cure for motion sickness and is thought to aid digestion.

Artichokes are a nice addition to this surprisingly easy version of the rustic Italian classic. This hearty recipe makes for a satisfying meal in a bowl (just double the serving size), or it can be served as a light appetizer. The soup keeps well in the freezer, so you can make a big batch to get you through those cold winter weekends.

MINESTRONE WITH ARTICHOKES
MAKES 8 (1-CUP) SERVINGS

12 ounces (3 links) lean Italian turkey sausage, sweet or spicy, casings removed

1 teaspoon olive oil

1 medium onion, chopped

1 tablespoon minced garlic

1 (14.5-ounce) can no-salt-added fire-roasted diced tomatoes or 1¾ cups chopped fresh tomatoes

1 large or 2 medium red bell peppers, roasted (see note, page 57), peeled, and diced

3 cups fat-free, low-sodium chicken broth

8 ounces (about 16) thawed frozen artichoke hearts, thinly sliced lengthwise

1 cup cooked farro, bulgur, or small whole wheat pasta (such as orzo or small shells)

1 cup cooked red or white kidney beans

1 teaspoon red chile flakes (optional) Salt and ground black pepper to taste

2 tablespoons chopped fresh basil

1 tablespoon grated Parmesan cheese

In a nonstick skillet, cook the sausage over medium heat for about 4 minutes, breaking it up with a spoon, until no longer pink. Drain the sausage on paper towels, crumble, and set aside.

In a 3- to 4-quart nonstick saucepan, heat the oil over medium-high heat. Add the onion and cook for about 4 minutes, or until soft and just starting to brown. Add the garlic and cook for 1 minute longer, until fragrant; do not brown the garlic. Add the tomatoes and roasted peppers and cook for 2 to 3 minutes.

Add the broth and bring to a boil. Reduce the heat to a simmer and add the artichoke hearts, cooked farro (or bulgur or pasta), and beans. Simmer for about 5 minutes, or until all the ingredients are heated through. Add the chile flakes, if desired, and season with salt and black pepper. Garnish with the basil and Parmesan.

Per serving: 160 calories, 4 g total fat (1 g saturated), 2 mg cholesterol, 440 mg sodium, 19 g total carbohydrates (4 g sugars), 6 g fiber, 12 g protein

You can use fresh grilled or seared tuna in this salad if you prefer, but canned tuna works just as well and makes this simple meal quick and easy to assemble. For a dish that more closely resembles the classic French salad, you can also substitute haricots verts for the asparagus.

SALADE NIÇOISE WITH CREAMY MUSTARD DRESSING

MAKES 4 (1-CUP) SERVINGS

4 ounces drained canned wild albacore or wild skipjack light tuna (I used Wild Planet brand)

½ pound asparagus, steamed or grilled and cut into 1½-inch pieces

2 hard-boiled eggs, finely diced

1 yellow bell pepper, roasted (see note, page 57), peeled, and diced

¼ cup (about 16) pitted kalamata olives or other intensely flavored olives, coarsely chopped

¼ cup Creamy Mustard Dressing (page 174)

Gently toss the tuna, asparagus, eggs, roasted pepper, and olives in a bowl.

Divide among 4 salad plates. Drizzle each salad with 1 tablespoon of the dressing.

Per serving: 150 calories, 8 g total fat (2 g saturated), 120 mg cholesterol, 480 mg sodium, 6 g total carbohydrates (2 g sugars), 2 g fiber, 14 g protein

---

A+ FOR ASPARAGUS

Like onions and leeks, asparagus is actually a member of the lily family. It's been prized as a delicacy since Greek and Roman times and is a good source of vitamin A. Asparagus' peak season is in spring and early summer; look for apple green stalks with tightly closed tips that are purplish to dark green. For optimal tenderness, cook asparagus the day you buy it or store it for a maximum of 4 days in the refrigerator.

This isn't a true ceviche, since I use cooked shrimp to make this easy appetizer, but the flavors are similar to those of a traditional shrimp ceviche. I like to serve this as a first course with a small green salad. It takes just minutes to prepare.

ALMOST CEVICHE

MAKES 4 SERVINGS

8	ounces canned wild shrimp, drained (I used Wild Planet brand)
1	ripe Hass avocado, diced
1	cup diced cucumber (unpeeled)
½	medium red bell pepper, diced
1–2	tablespoons chopped cilantro
⅓	cup Roasted Tomatillo Salsa (page 61) or your favorite salsa
2	teaspoons lime juice
1	teaspoon Chipotle Puree (page 192)
½	teaspoon Garlic Salt (page 193) or salt (optional)

Combine the shrimp, avocado, cucumber, bell pepper, and cilantro in a bowl and gently toss.

Combine the salsa, lime juice, and Chipotle Puree in a small bowl. Stir well and add to the shrimp mixture. Season with the Garlic Salt, if desired. Toss gently. Serve immediately or refrigerate for up to 1 day.

Per serving: 120 calories, 9 g total fat (<1 g saturated), 125 mg cholesterol, 300 mg sodium, 5 g total carbohydrates (1 g sugars), 2 g fiber, 13 g protein

NATURE'S HEALTHY FAT

Avocados are an excellent source of heart-healthy fats. Two phytosterols—beta-sitosterol and campesterol—simulate cholesterol's presence in the body, helping absorb fat-soluble vitamins and decreasing the amount of cholesterol the body produces and absorbs. In addition, the avocado's beautiful green color indicates the presence of the plant chemical lutein, which promotes eye health.

This flavorful soup answers the call when you have a craving for the sweet-savory taste of barbecue. The polenta and beans add some heft to the broth and increase the fiber and protein content of this dish. You can substitute lean beef or pork for the chicken, if you prefer—whatever the taste of "BBQ" means to you!

BBQ CHICKEN SOUP

MAKES 6 (1-CUP) SERVINGS

1 tablespoon canola or olive oil

1½ cups chopped yellow onions

1 tablespoon minced garlic

1 teaspoon ground cumin

3 cups fat-free, low-sodium chicken broth

1½ tablespoons polenta

8 ounces grilled boneless, skinless chicken breast, diced

1½ cups cooked beans (any type or combination—black beans, pinto, cannellini, etc.)

6 (½-ounce) slices nitrite-free turkey bacon, cooked and crumbled

½ cup barbecue sauce

¼ cup chopped cilantro

Chipotle Puree (page 192; optional)

In a 3-quart saucepan, heat the oil over medium-high heat. Add the onions and cook for 5 minutes, or until soft and just starting to brown. Add the garlic and cumin and cook for 1 minute longer, until the garlic is fragrant; do not brown the garlic.

Add the broth and bring to a boil. Whisk in the polenta and reduce the heat to a simmer. Stir in the beans, turkey bacon, barbecue sauce, cilantro, and Chipotle Puree, if desired. Simmer over low heat for 5 minutes or until heated through.

Per serving: 150 calories, 4 g total fat (0 g saturated), 10 mg cholesterol, 280 mg sodium, 22 g total carbohydrates (6 g sugars), 4 g fiber, 8 g protein

It takes only minutes to grate peeled, raw beets in a food processor. If you prefer, you can also use diced cooked beets, though the texture of raw beets gives this salad more volume and a bit of crunch.

SHREDDED BEETS WITH CRUMBLED FETA AND CREAMY CITRUS DRESSING

MAKES 8 ($1/2$-CUP) SERVINGS

4 cups grated raw beets (about 1$1/4$ pounds)

$1/4$ cup Citrus Vinaigrette (page 182)

2 tablespoons crumbled reduced-fat feta cheese

2 tablespoons chopped fresh chives

Toss the beets with the dressing. Top with the feta and chives. Serve at room temperature.

Per serving: 80 calories, 3 g total fat (0 g saturated), 20 mg cholesterol, 300 mg sodium, 12 g total carbohydrates (9 g sugars), 2 g fiber, 2 g protein

BEET IT

Antioxidant-rich beets have been cultivated for sugar production since the 17th century and have been consumed by humans for millennia. Beets come in a variety of jewel-toned hues, from garnet red to bright gold. To preserve their nutrient power, peel beets after cooking. And don't discard the greens, which also contain antioxidants in the form of chlorophyll and carotenoids. Save them for your next salad!

This recipe makes a gorgeous bowl of soup that's worthy of being served as the first course at a dinner party. It's also the perfect cure for a Tex-Mex craving—and because a serving is only 140 calories, you can have twice as much for a satisfying Mexican meal full of the flavors you love.

TORTILLA SOUP WITH AVOCADOS

MAKES 8 (1-CUP) SERVINGS

4	corn tortillas (6-inch diameter), halved and cut into 1/4-inch-wide strips
1	teaspoon canola or olive oil
1	medium yellow onion, chopped
1	tablespoon minced garlic
1	(14.5-ounce) can no-salt-added fire-roasted diced tomatoes
1	teaspoon chopped fresh oregano or 1/2 teaspoon dried
1	teaspoon ground cumin
5	cups fat-free, low-sodium chicken broth
1/2	cup diced carrots
1/3	cup diced roasted red bell pepper (see note, page 57)
1/3	cup diced roasted yellow bell pepper (see note, page 57)
1/3	cup diced celery
8	ounces honey-roasted or smoked turkey or chicken breast, diced
1/4	cup chopped cilantro
2	teaspoons grated lemon zest
	Salt and ground black pepper to taste (optional)
1	ripe Hass avocado, diced

Preheat the oven to 350°F. Lightly coat a baking sheet with cooking spray.

Place the tortilla strips on the sheet in a single layer. Bake until crisp and golden, turning once. Set aside.

In a 3-quart nonstick saucepan, heat the oil over medium heat. Add the onion and cook for 5 minutes, or until tender. Add the garlic and cook for 1 minute longer. Stir in the tomatoes, oregano, and cumin. Simmer for 10 minutes.

Add the broth and bring to a simmer. Add the carrots, roasted peppers, and celery. Cook for 3 minutes, or until tender. Add the turkey, cilantro, and lemon zest. Season with salt and black pepper, if desired. Divide among serving bowls and top with the avocado and tortilla strips.

Per serving: 140 calories, 5 g total fat (<1 g saturated), 25 mg cholesterol, 420 mg sodium, 13 g total carbohydrates (3 g sugars), 4 g fiber, 11 g protein

This delicious vegetable dish is made heartier by the addition of bacon and the smoky flavor of the grill. It makes a great side dish for a potluck or buffet.

GRILLED ROOT VEGETABLE SALAD WITH BACON AND CHIVES
MAKES 8 SERVINGS

2 pounds mixed root vegetables (such as sweet potatoes, squash, rutabagas, or turnips), peeled and cut into ½-inch-thick slices

1 medium yellow onion, cut crosswise into ½-inch-thick slices

1 red bell pepper, roasted (see note, page 57), peeled, and diced

6 (½-ounce) slices nitrite-free turkey bacon, cooked and crumbled

¼ cup chopped fresh chives or scallions

Prepare a medium fire in a charcoal grill or preheat a gas grill to medium. Lightly coat the grill rack (off the grill) with cooking spray and place over the hot fire. Lightly coat the top of the root vegetables, onion, and roasted pepper with cooking spray. Arrange all the vegetables on the oiled rack.

Grill the vegetables until tender, turning once, for about 10 minutes total. Remove from the grill and let cool for 5 minutes, or until cool enough to handle.

While the vegetables are grilling, combine the cooked bacon and chives or scallions in a medium bowl.

When the vegetables are cool enough to handle, cut them into ½-inch chunks. Add to the bowl and toss gently to combine. Serve immediately.

Per serving: 80 calories, 2 g total fat (0 g saturated), 10 mg cholesterol, 180 mg sodium, 14 g total carbohydrates (6 g sugars), 4 g fiber, 4 g protein

MEAT, FISH, AND POULTRY

From Thanksgiving turkey to burgers on the grill, the entrée, for most of us, is the course that defines the meal. Whether meat or vegetable, fish or fowl, we expect entrées to unite all the flavors on our plate and leave us feeling satisfied.

That seems like a tall order—but it's one that's surprisingly easy to fill. Even when you're trying to lose weight and eat healthfully, there's no need to limit yourself to bland baked or boiled entrées or to cut out red meat. In fact, the meat, poultry, and fish in most entrées supplies a vital source of your daily protein requirement. It's essential to get enough protein in your diet. Here are a few of protein's many benefits:

- Protein helps your body build and repair its tissues, including muscles, hair, skin, and blood vessels. If you work out a lot, it's especially important to get enough protein in your diet; it helps your muscles recover from tough workouts faster.

- A good source of essential nutrients, protein-rich foods deliver calcium, iron, selenium, and zinc, all of which are essential for building strong bones, fighting cancer, and protecting your immune system.

- When you eat a combination of protein and whole grains, you'll feel more satisfied than you would if you ate the grains alone. Combined with carbohydrates, proteins also help slow the release of sugars into the bloodstream, thereby preventing your blood sugar from spiking.

For all these reasons, roughly 30 percent of your calories should come from protein. But that goal isn't license to chow down on fried chicken and double burgers. Instead, focus on sources of high-quality protein—including vegetables—to create entrées that are as healthful as they are satisfying. A few strategies:

Choose meat wisely. Lean cuts of beef and pork are packed with protein and iron and are low in fat. Look for meats that are at least 90 percent lean; avoid marbled cuts of meat and ask your butcher to trim any fat off the edges. Since red meat tends to be higher in unhealthy saturated fat than other protein sources are, limit your intake to twice per week. Avoid eating processed meats such as bologna or hot dogs; they're high in fat, sodium, and calories and may contain carcinogenic sodium nitrites.

Eat naked poultry. White chicken and turkey meat are excellent sources of protein. But remove the skin before eating the poultry or cooking it in a recipe; doing so greatly reduces the fat and calorie content. Smart poultry choices also include turkey bacon and sausage (without nitrites), which are far leaner than most of their pork counterparts (except for the Italian Sausage Links on page 49!).

Go fish. In addition to supplying protein, seafood is rich in omega-3 fatty acids, vitamin E, and selenium, which can help prevent cancer and heart disease and may regulate thyroid function. Monitor portion sizes of cold-water fish such as salmon; they contain more heart-healthy fats than other types of seafood but are higher in calories, too.

Don't forget the veggies. As you've learned from making the delicious salads and soups in Chapter 4, robust, flavorful vegetables are more than worthy of taking center stage at mealtime.

The recipes on the following pages show how to combine cooking methods, spices, and sauces to create entrées that are both mouthwatering and healthy.

SALMON: KING OF HEALTHY FISH

Salmon contains omega-3 fatty acids, which are essential fats not produced by our bodies. Omega-3s are vital for brain function, healthy skin and hair, and well-tuned heart and nervous systems. Although omega-3s are also found in flaxseed, seaweed, and nuts, cold-water fish (such as wild salmon, mackerel, and herring) are the best sources of omega-3s. Types of salmon include:

- **Chinook or king salmon,** found in Pacific waters from Alaska to Southern California, can reach up to 120 pounds. A 4-ounce piece (raw) has about 200 calories and 2,300 milligrams of omega-3s.

- **Coho or silver salmon** are found in the Pacific as well as some freshwater lakes, such as the Great Lakes. A 4-ounce piece (raw) has 166 calories and 1,410 milligrams of omega-3s.

An aromatic combination of spices makes this pork dish a real showstopper. Pork tenderloin is as lean and nutritious as skinless chicken breast. Feel free to use bagged, preshredded cabbage and carrots to cut down on your prep time.

EASY PORK WITH GINGERED CURRY PASTE

MAKES 4 SERVINGS

2	teaspoons olive oil
1	pound pork tenderloin, cut into thin bite-size strips (see note on page 88)
1½	cups chopped yellow onions
1	tablespoon chopped garlic
1	tablespoon chopped fresh ginger
1	teaspoon turmeric
1	teaspoon garam masala or curry powder
¾	teaspoon ground cumin
½	teaspoon ground coriander
1	medium red bell pepper, roasted (see note, page 57), peeled, and diced
2½	cups shredded green cabbage
½	cup grated carrots
1½	cups fat-free, low-sodium chicken broth
½	cup finely diced prunes, dried currants, or raisins
¼	cup chopped cilantro + leaves for garnish
2	cups cooked brown or wild rice (optional)

In a nonstick skillet, heat 1 teaspoon of the oil over medium-high heat. Add the pork and cook, stirring for about 2 minutes to brown. Remove from the pan and set aside.

Reduce the heat to medium and add the remaining 1 teaspoon oil to the skillet. Add the onions and cook for about 5 minutes, or until soft and just starting to brown. Add the garlic, ginger, and spices and cook for a few minutes, or until fragrant.

Add the roasted pepper, cabbage, carrots, and broth to the pan. Reduce the heat to low, cover, and cook for about 5 minutes, or until the cabbage is wilted. Stir in the dried fruit and chopped cilantro. Place the pork on top of the cabbage, cover, and cook for about 3 minutes longer, or until the pork is just cooked through.

(continued)

Divide the rice (if desired) among 4 plates. Top with the pork and vegetables. Garnish with cilantro leaves.

Note: To slice pork more easily into thin strips, pop the tenderloin in the freezer for 20 to 30 minutes before slicing. Cut the tenderloin crosswise into thin slices, then cut each slice into thin strips.

Per serving with rice: 390 calories, 9 g total fat (2 g saturated), 75 mg cholesterol, 250 mg sodium, 47 g total carbohydrates (13 g sugars), 6 g fiber, 30 g protein

Per serving without rice: 280 calories, 8 g total fat (2 g saturated), 75 mg cholesterol, 250 mg sodium, 25 g total carbohydrates (13 g sugars), 4 g fiber, 27 g protein

THE OTHER WHITE MEAT

For once, there's truth in advertising! The popular slogan suggests that pork can be as healthy as poultry. And, in fact, lean pork tenderloin stacks up well compared with turkey or chicken breast. A 3-ounce serving has 112 calories, 18 grams of protein, and 4 grams of fat. And it's easy to prepare, from a quick stir-fry to marinating and grilling to slow-cooking.

When the weather turns cool, who doesn't love curling up with a warm bowl of chili? This recipe freezes well and yields a large batch—enough for family dinners throughout the week. If you have just a cup or so leftover, you can use it as a topping for your favorite baked chips for an instant, healthy nacho snack.

FIRE-ROASTED CHILI

MAKES 9 (1-CUP) SERVINGS

1 tablespoon canola or olive oil

1½ cups chopped onions

1 tablespoon chopped garlic

1¼ pounds (20 ounces) extra-lean ground turkey or beef

2 red bell peppers, roasted (see note, page 57), peeled, and diced

1 tablespoon + 1 teaspoon chili powder

1½ teaspoons ground cumin

1 teaspoon ground coriander

1 teaspoon ground mustard

½ teaspoon dried oregano

2 (14.5-ounce) cans no-salt-added fire-roasted diced tomatoes

2 cups fat-free, low-sodium chicken broth

1½ cups cooked black beans or 1 (16-ounce) can, rinsed and drained

½ cup diced pitted prunes

¼ cup chopped cilantro

1–2 teaspoons Chipotle Puree (page 192) or red chile flakes (optional)

Salt to taste (optional)

In a 4-quart saucepan, heat the oil over medium heat. Add the onions and cook for about 5 minutes, or until soft. Add the garlic and cook for 1 minute longer; do not brown the garlic. Add the turkey or beef and cook until no longer pink.

Add the roasted peppers, chili powder, cumin, coriander, mustard, and oregano. Cook over medium-high heat, stirring occasionally, for 2 minutes. Add the tomatoes and broth and bring to a boil. Reduce the heat and simmer uncovered for 5 minutes.

Stir in the beans, prunes, and cilantro. Continue cooking for an additional 2 minutes or until just heated through. Season with Chipotle Puree and salt, if desired.

Per serving: 190 calories, 3 g total fat (<1 g saturated), 25 mg cholesterol, 240 mg sodium, 21 g total carbohydrates (7 g sugars), 5 g fiber, 19 g protein

Ratatouille is a classic Provençal dish consisting of slowly simmered eggplant, bell peppers, tomatoes, onions, and fresh herbs. In this rendition, these traditional ingredients are first cooked on the grill for added smoky flavor.

SMOKY RATATOUILLE WITH SPICY SAUSAGE

MAKES 4 SERVINGS

2   (4-ounce) links spicy Italian turkey sausage

1   medium white or red onion, sliced into $\frac{1}{2}$-inch-thick rings

3   zucchini (yellow or green), cut lengthwise into $\frac{1}{2}$-inch-thick slices

1   eggplant (about 1$\frac{1}{2}$ pounds), cut lengthwise into $\frac{1}{2}$-inch-thick slices

2   red, yellow, or green bell peppers, roasted (see note, page 57), peeled, and cut into $\frac{1}{2}$-inch squares

1   (14.5-ounce) can no-salt-added fire-roasted diced tomatoes (see note)

1   tablespoon grated lemon zest

1   tablespoon chopped fresh basil

1   teaspoon chopped fresh thyme

    Salt and ground black pepper (optional)

2   tablespoons chopped flat-leaf (Italian) parsley, for garnish

Remove the sausage meat from the casings. Cook in a nonstick skillet over medium-high heat until no longer pink. Drain and crumble the sausage.

Prepare a grill and heat to medium-high heat (when the fire is ready, you can hold your hand 5 inches above the rack for no longer than 3 to 4 seconds). Insert a toothpick horizontally through each onion slice, going through all the rings to the center to hold the slices intact. Lightly coat the onion, zucchini, and eggplant with olive oil cooking spray. Grill the vegetables on the grill rack, turning once, until done, about 4 minutes total. (The onions may take longer.)

When cool enough to handle, cut the grilled vegetables into $\frac{1}{2}$-inch dice and transfer to a bowl. Add the roasted peppers, tomatoes, lemon zest, basil, and thyme. Stir in the sausage. Season with salt and black pepper, if desired. Transfer to a serving bowl and garnish with the parsley.

Note: You can substitute 1 pound grape or cherry tomatoes (yellow or red) for the fire-roasted tomatoes. Grill fresh tomatoes on skewers, carefully turning, until they are softened and the skins just begin to split.

Per serving: 170 calories, 6 g total fat (2 g saturated), 35 mg cholesterol, 389 mg sodium, 21 g total carbohydrates (11 g sugars), 8 g fiber, 12 g protein

This recipe perfectly exemplifies the saying "a little goes a long way." The flavor of toasted sesame oil is highly intense—not much is needed to impart major flavor. If you don't eat shellfish, you could substitute bite-size pieces of fish such as salmon or flounder.

SESAME PRAWNS
MAKES 4 SERVINGS

¼   cup coarsely chopped cilantro

2   tablespoons chopped fresh mint leaves

2   scallions, coarsely chopped

1   tablespoon chopped fresh ginger

2   cloves garlic

½   teaspoon red chile flakes (optional)

3   tablespoons + ½ cup fat-free, low-sodium chicken broth

1   tablespoon canola or olive oil

1   cup coarsely chopped yellow onion

1   medium red bell pepper, diced

1   medium yellow bell pepper, diced

1½ teaspoons toasted sesame oil

1   pound prawns or jumbo shrimp, peeled and deveined

¼   cup low-sodium soy sauce
    Salt and ground black pepper to taste

2   teaspoons toasted sesame seeds (see note), for garnish

2   cups cooked wild or brown rice

Combine the cilantro, mint, scallions, ginger, garlic, chile flakes (if desired), and 3 tablespoons of the broth in a food processor. Pulse until the mixture is minced but not pureed. Set aside.

In a large nonstick skillet, heat the canola oil over medium-high heat. Add the onion and bell peppers and cook for 5 minutes, or until just tender. Transfer to a bowl and cover to retain the heat.

Add the sesame oil to the skillet and place over medium-high heat. Add the cilantro mixture and cook for about 1 minute, stirring constantly. Add the remaining ½ cup broth and bring to a boil. Add the prawns and soy sauce and cook for 2 minutes, or until the prawns are just cooked. Return the onion-pepper mixture to the skillet and stir for 1 minute to heat through. Season with salt and black pepper. Garnish with toasted sesame seeds and serve with warm wild rice.

Note: Toast sesame seeds on a baking sheet in an oven preheated to 350°F for about 10 minutes, rotating the baking sheet halfway through.

Per serving: 290 calories, 8 g total fat (1 g saturated), 170 mg cholesterol, 250 mg sodium, 27 g total carbohydrates (4 g sugars), 4 g fiber, 28 g protein

290 CALORIES

This slow-cooker dish is so easy to make and so delicious. If you don't have Spicy Caribbean Barbecue Sauce in the fridge (or don't have time to make it), you can substitute any store-bought brand of low-sugar barbecue sauce.

BEER-BRAISED PORK TACOS

MAKES 4 (2-TACO) SERVINGS

2 teaspoons olive or canola oil

1 pound pork tenderloin

1 cup finely chopped onion

½ cup finely chopped carrot

1 teaspoon chopped garlic

1 cup beer (any variety)

1 cup Spicy Caribbean Barbecue Sauce (page 178) + additional for serving (optional)

8 corn tortillas (6-inch diameter)

2 tablespoons chopped cilantro, for garnish

Chipotle Puree (optional; page 192)

In a nonstick skillet, heat the oil over medium-high heat. Quickly brown the pork and transfer it to a slow cooker. Add the onion and carrot to the skillet and cook for about 5 minutes, or until soft and just starting to brown. Add the garlic and cook for 1 minute longer. Add the beer and 1 cup barbecue sauce and bring just to a boil. Remove from the heat and pour over the pork.

Cover the slow cooker and cook on high for about 3 hours. The pork will be very tender and will separate easily with a fork.

Wrap the tortillas in foil and warm in the oven at a low temperature for about 15 minutes. Serve the pork in the warm tortillas garnished with cilantro. Pass Chipotle Puree and extra barbecue sauce in squeeze bottles, if desired.

Per serving: 340 calories, 5 g total fat (2 g saturated), 75 mg cholesterol, 135 mg sodium, 41 g total carbohydrates (9 g sugars), 6 g fiber, 28 g protein

This dish makes a stunning centerpiece for your holiday table, and your guests would never guess that it's less than 150 calories per serving. Serve these pretty slices of roulade with extra dressing, Porcini Mushroom Gravy (page 184), and Warm Apple and Cranberry Sauce (page 187).

TURKEY ROULADE WITH CORNBREAD AND DRIED FRUIT DRESSING

MAKES 8 (2-SLICE) SERVINGS

½ boneless, skinless turkey breast (about 1½ pounds)

1½ cups uncooked Cornbread and Dried Fruit Dressing (page 118)

¼ teaspoon dried marjoram

¼ teaspoon dried thyme

¼ teaspoon crumbled sage

¼ teaspoon smoked paprika

¼ teaspoon ground black pepper

1 tablespoon canola oil

Preheat the oven to 350°F.

Place a very large piece of plastic wrap on the countertop. Place the turkey breast half on the plastic and cover with additional plastic wrap. Using a meat mallet, pound the turkey breast to a rectangle 9–10 × 6 inches, about ¼ inch thick.

Remove the plastic wrap and spread the cornbread dressing evenly over the surface. Roll the turkey breast lengthwise. With kitchen twine, tie the roulade lengthwise once and in several places across the turkey.

In a small bowl, mix together the herbs and spices. Rub the oil evenly over the roulade, then rub with the herb-spice blend.

Place the roulade in a shallow roasting pan and roast for 45 to 60 minutes, or until the internal temperature measured with an instant-read thermometer reads 155°F. Remove from the oven and let rest for 15 minutes before carefully removing the twine and slicing into sixteen ½-inch slices (2 per person).

Per serving: 140 calories, 4 g total fat (<1 g saturated), 65 mg cholesterol, 150 mg sodium, 5 g total carbohydrates (1 g sugars), 0 g fiber, 22 g protein

Cooking "en papillote" means sealing the ingredients in a paper or foil packet, which traps both steam and flavor inside. The packets can be assembled a few hours ahead of time and popped in the oven just before dinner. You can substitute an equal weight of shrimp or scallops.

SALMON EN PAPILLOTE WITH TOMATOES AND FENNEL

MAKES 4 SERVINGS

2	teaspoons extra-virgin olive oil
1	medium bulb fennel, trimmed, quartered lengthwise, cored, and sliced
1	small red onion, halved and thinly sliced
1½	cups cherry or grape tomatoes, halved lengthwise
1	tablespoon minced garlic
1	tablespoon chopped fresh basil or 1 teaspoon dried
4	salmon fillets (5 ounces each)

In a nonstick skillet, heat the oil over medium-high heat. Add the fennel and onion and cook for about 4 minutes, or until they're just beginning to soften. Add the tomatoes, garlic, and basil and cook for 2 minutes longer. Remove from the heat and set aside.

Preheat the oven to 400°F.

Cut off four 15 × 15-inch squares of parchment paper or foil. Fold a square of parchment in half to create a crease, and then open up. Place a fish fillet on one side of the crease. Repeat for the remaining fillets. Top each of the fillets with one-fourth of the veggie mixture. Fold the edges of the paper together and then tightly fold in the edges, crimping around all sides to seal the packets completely. Place the packets on a baking sheet. Bake for 10 to 12 minutes, until the fish flakes easily with a fork.

Place each packet on a dinner plate. To serve, slit the packet with an X and fold back the paper.

Per serving: 260 calories, 10 g total fat (2 g saturated), 65 mg cholesterol, 95 mg sodium, 9 g total carbohydrates (2 g sugars), 3 g fiber, 33 g protein

GRAINS AND LEGUMES

Whole grains and legumes such as beans are the unsung heroes of a healthy diet. They may not have the eye-popping appeal of brilliantly colored fruits and vegetables, the hearty sizzle of a steak, or the rich texture of salmon, but they're versatile, inexpensive, easy to prepare—and packed with both flavor and a variety of health benefits.

WHOLE GRAINS

Whole grains have gotten a bad rap in recent years, as the pendulum of diet fads has swung away from carbohydrates in general. It's true that refined carbohydrates—the "white stuff," such as white bread, pasta, potatoes, and pastries—can cause blood sugar and insulin levels in the body to spike quickly, which can lead to weight gain and even metabolic disorders. But your body relies on stored carbohydrate, called glycogen, to build and repair muscle; without it, your body burns stored fat, initiating a process called ketosis, which can stress the kidneys and liver.

Not only do our bodies need the carbohydrates contained in whole grains for energy, but grains also deliver powerful nutrients and antioxidants that bolster immunity, help prevent cancer and heart disease, and slow aging.

Whole grains are nutritious because, unlike refined grains, all parts of the plant have been left intact, including the fiber-rich outer layer of the kernel, called the bran, and the vitamin-rich seed, which is called the germ. Refining and processing often remove these two crucial parts of the grain,

leaving only the largest part, the endosperm, which supplies protein and carbohydrate. The more highly refined the grain, the higher the percentage of simple carbohydrate remaining—simple carbohydrate rapidly converts to blood sugar, or glucose. For example, whole wheat flour contains 13.3 percent protein and 71 percent carbohydrate, while extensively refined and milled cake flour contains 7.5 percent protein and 79.4 percent carbohydrate.

But the world of whole grains goes well beyond bakery goods and pastas made from whole wheat flour. Grains such as barley, bulgur, quinoa, polenta, and brown and wild rice lend unique textures and flavors to recipes and can be incorporated into both sweet and savory dishes.

LEGUMES: NUTRITION SUPERSTARS

Like whole grains, legumes—beans, lentils, peas, soybeans, and other seed pod plants—are high in antioxidants and fiber. They're also a good source of folate, an essential nutrient that helps prevent birth defects and lowers levels of homocysteine, an amino acid in the blood. Although results from recent clinical trials are mixed, lowering homocysteine may reduce the risk of heart disease.

In addition, legumes are loaded with protein, making them a good alternative to meat, which is higher in calories and fat. An entire cup of cooked black beans has only 225 calories and 1 gram of fat, but 16 grams of protein. By comparison, a 6-ounce serving of lean broiled sirloin has 51.6 grams of protein—but also packs 316 calories and a whopping 10.6 grams of fat, almost half of it unhealthy saturated fat.

Most dried beans require presoaking (you can soak them overnight) for several hours to reduce cooking time. I prefer cooking my own legumes, as their flavors remain rich when freshly cooked. But if you're on the go, canned beans can be just as healthy, and an increasing variety of canned beans are available in the grocery store. Just be sure to choose low-sodium versions.

Unlike beans, lentils require no soaking and can usually be prepared in less than an hour. Like beans, lentils are legumes—but because the disk-shaped lentil seeds are small, they cook much more quickly. Lentils are also a nutrient powerhouse:

They're not only high in fiber, iron, and protein (like other legumes), but they also contain stores of potassium, magnesium, and vitamin B_1 (thiamin), which helps keep nerves and muscle tissue healthy.

GRAINS AND LEGUMES: A PERFECT PROTEIN PAIR

Legumes are an excellent source of protein, but only soybeans are considered a "complete" protein—meaning they contain all nine amino acids essential to building protein in the body. Other beans, along with nuts and seeds, are "incomplete" proteins, meaning they lack one or more of those amino acids.

But the good news is that whole grains make up for what legumes lack, and together they make a complete protein factory. Maybe that's why so many cultures across the globe pair legumes and grains—think of classic dishes like rice and beans, rice and lentils, or corn and bean salsa. Each of these dishes offers a near-perfect combination of nutrients.

In addition to being essential parts of a healthy diet, whole grains and legumes are also simple to prepare and—as you'll find out yourself when you make the recipes in this chapter—absolutely delicious.

The bright colors and flavors of fresh vegetables shine in this simple pasta dish. The hearty texture of whole grain pasta combined with protein-rich legumes makes for a light yet satisfying meal that's packed with nutrition . . . and flavor, of course!

RIGATONI WITH WHITE BEANS AND WILTED CHARD

MAKES 4 (¾-CUP) SERVINGS

2   teaspoons olive oil

1   cup halved cherry tomatoes or drained canned no-salt-added fire-roasted diced tomatoes

1   tablespoon chopped garlic

1   (15.5-ounce) can cannellini or great Northern white beans, rinsed and drained

¾   cup fat-free, low-sodium chicken broth

3   cups chopped Swiss chard or 1½ cups thawed frozen spinach

¼   teaspoon ground black pepper

½   teaspoon salt (optional)

4   ounces dry whole wheat rigatoni pasta, cooked until al dente

2   tablespoons grated Parmesan cheese

1   tablespoon chopped fresh basil

In a 3-quart saucepan, heat the oil over medium heat. Add the tomatoes and garlic and cook for about 3 minutes, or until the tomatoes are tender. Add the beans and broth and bring to a boil. Add the chard, pepper, and salt, if desired, and cook for about 2 minutes, or until the chard just begins to wilt.

Add the pasta, coat well, and cook until heated through.

Serve hot, topped with the Parmesan and basil.

Per serving: 140 calories, 4 g total fat (1 g saturated), 0 mg cholesterol, 385 mg sodium, 24 g total carbohydrates (2 g sugars), 5 g fiber, 6 g protein

This versatile pasta dish is easy to assemble and lends itself well to variation. Try it with different herbs, add fresh spinach, or replace the tomatoes with cooked mushrooms. Any way you choose to make it, you'll find that it turns your everyday dinner into something special.

LEMONY ORZO WITH FIRE-ROASTED TOMATOES

MAKES 6 SERVINGS

2 teaspoons olive oil

1 (14.5-ounce) can no-salt-added fire-roasted diced tomatoes

⅓ cup finely diced onion

1 teaspoon minced garlic

1 cup (6 ounces) whole wheat orzo (see Shopping Sources/Grains, Nuts, and Legumes, page 200)

1½ cups fat-free, low-sodium chicken or vegetable broth

1 tablespoon chopped fresh basil

1 tablespoon finely chopped pine nuts

1 tablespoon grated Romano cheese

2 teaspoons finely chopped capers

1 teaspoon grated lemon zest

½ teaspoon red chile flakes (optional)

¼ teaspoon salt

¼ teaspoon ground black pepper

1 tablespoon chopped flat-leaf (Italian) parsley, for garnish

In a medium skillet, heat the oil over medium heat. Add the tomatoes, onion, and garlic and cook for 3 minutes, or until tender. Set tomato sauce aside.

In a 2-quart saucepan, combine the orzo and broth and bring to a boil over medium-high heat. Reduce the heat to a simmer, cover, and cook according to package directions or until the orzo is al dente. Remove from the heat and let stand about 3 minutes, or until almost all the liquid is absorbed.

Stir in the basil, pine nuts, Romano, capers, lemon zest, chile flakes (if desired), salt, and black pepper until just combined. Stir in the tomato sauce. Garnish with the parsley and serve hot.

Per serving: 150 calories, 3 g total fat (0 g saturated), 0 mg cholesterol, 216 mg sodium, 24 g total carbohydrates (3 g sugars), 5 g fiber, 5 g protein

This rich, gooey side dish is loaded with veggies and is big on flavor. If you like your "rotini 'n' cheese" a little spicy, be sure to add the Chipotle Puree. Serve with grilled chicken or fish and a simple green salad for a healthy meal.

CREAMY FOUR-CHEESE PASTA

MAKES 6 (SCANT 1-CUP) SERVINGS

¼ cup white whole wheat flour (I used King Arthur brand)

1½ cups 1% milk

1 cup shredded reduced-fat Mexican 4-cheese blend

1 teaspoon Worcestershire sauce

1 teaspoon Chipotle Puree (page 192) or red chile flakes (optional)

3 cups cooked whole grain rotini (about 5 ounces dry)

1 cup steamed, chopped spinach or 1 cup thawed frozen spinach, drained

1 red bell pepper, roasted (see note, page 57), peeled, and diced, or ½ cup fire-roasted diced tomatoes or fresh salsa

2 tablespoons minced shallots or ¼ cup minced yellow onion

Salt and ground black pepper to taste

Preheat the oven to 375°F.

In a 3- to 4-quart saucepan, whisk together the flour and ½ cup of the milk until smooth. Whisk in the remaining 1 cup milk and place the pan over medium heat. Bring to a boil and simmer, stirring constantly, for about 10 minutes, or until thick. Whisk in the cheese until melted. Stir in the Worcestershire sauce and Chipotle Puree or chile flakes, if desired.

Remove the pan from the heat and fold in the cooked pasta, spinach, roasted pepper (or diced tomatoes or salsa), and shallots or onion. Season with salt and black pepper.

Lightly coat a 1½-quart baking dish with cooking spray. Pour the pasta mixture into the dish. Bake for 30 minutes, or until bubbling.

Per serving: 200 calories, 5 g total fat (2 g saturated), 15 mg cholesterol, 200 mg sodium, 29 g total carbohydrates (4 g sugars), 5 g fiber, 13 g protein

POPEYE WAS (SORT OF) RIGHT

Spinach is a good source of fiber and is rich in vitamin C and beta-carotene, which the body converts to vitamin A. It also contains iron and calcium, but spinach's oxalic acid content inhibits the absorption of these two minerals. So while Popeye doubtless gained immunity and strength from the vitamins in spinach, he didn't get much iron!

A simple combination of fresh herbs, grated lemon, and toasted nuts turns an everyday veggie into something elegant. The Medjool dates add a hint of sweetness and complement the earthy flavor of pumpkin.

PEARL COUSCOUS WITH ROASTED PUMPKIN AND MEDJOOL DATES

MAKES 8 (¾-CUP) SERVINGS

2 tablespoons finely chopped Medjool dates or prunes

2 tablespoons chopped walnuts, toasted

2 tablespoons grated Parmigiano-Reggiano cheese

1 tablespoon chopped flat-leaf (Italian) parsley or ½ teaspoon dried

2 teaspoons grated lemon zest

5 cups diced pumpkin or winter squash, such as Hubbard or kabocha (about 1¼ pounds)

4 large shallots, quartered lengthwise

2 teaspoons canola oil

1¼ cups fat-free, low-sodium chicken broth

½ teaspoon salt (optional)

¼ teaspoon ground cumin

¼ teaspoon ground cinnamon

1 cup whole wheat Israeli pearl couscous

2 tablespoons chopped cilantro, for garnish

Combine the dates or prunes, walnuts, cheese, parsley, and lemon zest in a small bowl. Set aside.

Preheat the oven to 425°F.

Combine the pumpkin or squash, shallots, and oil in a medium bowl and toss well. Transfer to a baking sheet. Roast for about 30 minutes, stirring occasionally, until the pumpkin starts to brown but is still holding its shape.

Combine the broth, salt (if desired), cumin, and cinnamon in a Dutch oven and bring to a boil. Add the couscous. Stir to coat, cover, and simmer for 5 to 10 minutes, or as directed on the couscous package. When the couscous is cooked, add the roasted vegetables and date mixture and toss gently to combine. Garnish with the cilantro. Serve hot.

Per serving: 170 calories, 3 g total fat (<1 g saturated), 0 mg cholesterol, 230 mg sodium, 32 g total carbohydrates (5 g sugars), 6 g fiber, 6 g protein

This vegetable "lasagna" is really easy to make, and you can use whatever mushrooms you prefer. This makes a gorgeous first course or side dish.

PASTICCIATA (POLENTA LASAGNA) WITH GARLIC SPINACH AND MUSHROOMS

MAKES 4 SERVINGS

POLENTA

1 (24-ounce) tube precooked, ready-to-heat polenta

MUSHROOMS

2 teaspoons olive oil

1 medium yellow onion, chopped

6 ounces white or brown mushrooms, cleaned and sliced (3 cups)

1 teaspoon chopped fresh thyme or 1/2 teaspoon dried

1 cup fat-free, low-sodium chicken broth

2 tablespoons grated Parmigiano-Reggiano cheese

1/4 teaspoon ground nutmeg

SPINACH

2 teaspoons olive oil

1 tablespoon chopped garlic

1 (12-ounce) bag spinach

1/2 teaspoon salt

1/2 teaspoon ground black pepper

Sprig of thyme or flat-leaf (Italian) parsley, for garnish

To make the polenta: Preheat the oven to 400°F. Cut the polenta into twelve 1/2-inch slices. Coat lightly with cooking spray and place on a baking sheet. Bake for 8 minutes, then turn the polenta slices and bake for 8 minutes longer. Remove from the oven and keep warm.

To make the mushrooms: In a large skillet, heat the oil over medium heat. Add the onion and cook for about 7 minutes. Add the mushrooms and thyme and cook, stirring often, for about 2 minutes. Carefully add the broth and bring to a boil. Immediately reduce the heat to low and simmer for 10 minutes, until the mixture is reduced. Stir in the cheese and nutmeg. Remove from the heat. Cover to keep warm.

To make the spinach: In a large skillet, heat the oil over medium-high heat. Add the garlic and then the spinach (do not let the garlic brown). Turn the spinach until wilted and just cooked. Season with salt and pepper.

To serve: Transfer the spinach to a warmed serving dish and spread out in an even layer. Arrange the polenta slices on top of the spinach and top with the mushrooms. Garnish with the herbs.

Per serving: 220 calories, 6 g total fat (1 g saturated), 20 mg cholesterol, 350 mg sodium, 34 g total carbohydrates (4 g sugars), 4 g fiber, 9 g protein

This dish is loaded with protein, fiber, and flavor. It's a great accompaniment alongside roasted chicken or pork. If you use canned black-eyed peas, be sure to rinse them first to wash away most of the added sodium.

BLACK-EYED PEAS WITH GREENS AND HAM

MAKES 8 (½-CUP) SERVINGS

1 tablespoon olive oil

1 cup chopped onion

¼ cup finely chopped carrot

¼ cup finely chopped celery

4 (1-ounce) slices Canadian bacon, diced

1 tablespoon minced garlic

1 teaspoon ground mustard

1 teaspoon fresh oregano or ½ teaspoon dried

3 cups cooked black-eyed peas

1 cup beer

2 cups coarsely chopped mustard greens, Swiss chard, or spinach

1 tablespoon balsamic vinegar

In a large skillet, heat the oil over medium heat. Add the onion, carrot, and celery and cook for 8 minutes, or until the vegetables become tender and just start to brown. Stir in the bacon, garlic, mustard, and oregano and cook for 1 minute.

Add the black-eyed peas and beer. Bring to a boil, reduce the heat, and simmer for 20 minutes. Add the greens to the pan and stir well. Cover and simmer for 5 minutes, or until they're tender and wilted. Stir in the vinegar. Serve hot.

Per serving: 140 calories, 3 g total fat (1 g saturated), 10 mg cholesterol, 125 mg sodium, 18 g total carbohydrates (3 g sugars), 5 g fiber, 9 g protein

---

CHARD: A MIGHTY GREEN

Chard, also called Swiss chard, comes in green or red varieties, both of which are flavorful, easy to find, easy to prepare, and easy on the pocketbook. Though it's delicious on its own, the leaves can be torn or shredded and stirred into a soup or a grain dish for extra color, flavor, and texture. Chard is loaded with vitamins: One cup of cooked chard delivers 210 percent of your recommended daily vitamin A, 50 percent of vitamin C, 4 grams of fiber, and only 35 calories.

This is one of the few recipes in this book that take a little extra time to prepare and call for a specialized piece of equipment. But once you taste the homemade mushroom pasta, you won't have a single regret about the extra minutes you spent in the kitchen.

MUSHROOM PASTA WITH RAPINI AND PARMESAN

MAKES 4 SERVINGS

Mushroom Pasta (page 116)

1 tablespoon olive oil

2 tablespoons diced shallots

4 ounces cremini, brown, or chanterelle mushrooms, coarsely chopped

6 shiitake mushrooms, stems discarded and caps sliced

½ cup fat-free, low-sodium chicken or vegetable broth

Salt and ground black pepper

8 ounces rapini (broccoli rabe) or broccoli, cut into 2-inch lengths and blanched

2 tablespoons grated Parmesan cheese

2 tablespoons chopped flat-leaf (Italian) parsley, for garnish

Make the pasta. Bring a large pot of water to a rolling boil.

Meanwhile, in a large skillet, heat the oil over medium heat. Add the shallots and mushrooms and cook for 5 minutes, or until they are soft but not browned. Add the broth and stir in salt and pepper to taste. Reduce the heat to low.

Add 1 teaspoon of salt to the boiling water, add the pasta, and cook for 2 to 3 minutes, or until al dente. Watch the pasta carefully, because it cooks quickly. Drain the pasta and return to the pot.

Add the rapini or broccoli and mushrooms to the hot pasta and toss well. Serve topped with the Parmesan and some parsley.

Per serving: 340 calories, 8 g total fat (2 g saturated), 165 mg cholesterol, 330 mg sodium, 48 g total carbohydrates (2 g sugars), 9 g fiber, 16 g protein

MUSHROOM PASTA

You can substitute other dried mushrooms for the porcinis, if you prefer.

MAKES ENOUGH FOR 4 SERVINGS

1½ cups white whole wheat flour
(I used King Arthur brand)

1 ounce dried porcini mushrooms, ground
to a fine powder in a spice grinder
(about ½ cup)

¾ teaspoon salt-free Italian seasoning

½ teaspoon salt

3 large eggs, preferably omega-3-enriched

Combine the flour, porcini powder, Italian seasoning, and salt in a bowl. Pour the mixture out onto a clean work surface into a mound. Create a large well in the center and crack the eggs into the well.

Gradually incorporate the flour mixture from the sides of the well into the eggs. Work the ingredients together until it forms a rough and sticky ball. If the dough is too sticky, add a small amount of flour. If the dough is too dry, add a few drops of cold water.

Scrape the dough off the work surface, press into a rough ball, and knead for about 5 minutes. The dough should be very smooth and elastic. There will be about 14 ounces of pasta dough.

Shape the dough in a ball and wrap tightly in plastic wrap. Let rest for 20 minutes at room temperature.

Unwrap the ball of dough and cut into 4 pieces. Put 3 pieces back into the plastic wrap so that they don't dry out. Flatten the remaining piece of dough into a rough rectangle.

Following the manufacturer's instructions for your pasta machine, feed the flattened piece of dough into the machine at the widest setting. Fold the dough into thirds and then feed again into the machine. Repeat folding and rolling two additional times. Decrease the roller setting 1 notch. Sprinkle the pasta lightly with flour if necessary (may not be needed) and feed through the rollers again, unfolded. Turn the roller setting another notch and repeat the rolling, then continue without folding the dough until you get to the 5th setting. Repeat with the remaining pieces of dough. Cut the pasta into tagliatelle or fettuccine. Repeat with the other 3 pieces of dough.

Per serving: 260 calories, 4 g total fat (1 g saturated), 160 mg cholesterol, 360 mg sodium, 40 g total carbohydrates (0 g sugars), 8 g fiber, 12 g protein

Stuffing that's prepared separately from the meat of a dish is actually called dressing. Since it's not cooked inside the cavity of the bird, it can become dry if you don't add enough moisture. But this dressing is luscious and moist, and it doesn't contain any of the cholesterol and fat that's absorbed when stuffing is baked inside a turkey.

CORNBREAD AND DRIED FRUIT DRESSING

MAKES 8 ($\frac{1}{2}$-CUP) SERVINGS

4 cups cornbread cubes, dried

4 ounces lean Italian turkey sausage, casings removed (or 3 Italian Sausage Links, page 49)

1 tablespoon canola oil

1 cup chopped yellow or white onion

$\frac{1}{4}$ cup diced celery

$\frac{1}{4}$ cup diced carrot

1 small clove garlic, crushed through a press

4 dried apricots, coarsely chopped

4 pitted prunes, coarsely chopped

$\frac{3}{4}$ teaspoon dried sage

$\frac{1}{2}$ teaspoon dried thyme

$\frac{1}{4}$ teaspoon dried marjoram

1 cup fat-free, low-sodium chicken broth

$\frac{1}{4}$ cup minced parsley

$\frac{1}{2}$ teaspoon salt

$\frac{1}{4}$ teaspoon ground black pepper

1 egg, lightly beaten

Preheat the oven to 350°F. Place the cornbread in a large heatproof bowl and set aside. In a small nonstick skillet, cook the sausage over medium-high heat, crumbling and stirring, until browned and cooked through. Drain well and set aside.

In a large nonstick skillet, heat the oil over medium heat. Stir in the onion, celery, and carrot and cook for 5 minutes, stirring frequently. Add the garlic and cook for 1 minute longer; do not let the garlic brown. Stir in the sausage, apricots, prunes, sage, thyme, marjoram, and $\frac{1}{4}$ cup of the broth and bring to a boil. Reduce the heat and simmer for 3 minutes. Remove from the heat and pour over the cornbread. Add the parsley and stir well. Season with the salt and pepper. (The dressing may be prepared to this stage a day ahead and refrigerated, covered.)

Whisk together the egg and remaining $\frac{3}{4}$ cup broth and pour over the cornbread mixture, tossing well. Coat a 2-quart baking dish with cooking spray. Transfer the cornbread mixture to the baking dish. Cover with foil and bake for about 30 minutes, or until the top begins to brown.

Per serving: 100 calories, 4 g total fat (1 g saturated), 30 mg cholesterol, 310 mg sodium, 12 g total carbohydrates (4 g sugars), 1 g fiber, 3 g protein

Loaded with protein and fiber, this exotic-tasting bean dish is scrumptious and filling. It can be served as a main course or in $^1/_2$-cup side dish portions with grilled chicken or shrimp. Don't let leftover coconut milk go to waste—it can be frozen for later use in smoothies or desserts.

CARIBBEAN BEANS AND RICE

MAKES 10 ($^1/_2$-CUP) SERVINGS

2   teaspoons canola or olive oil

1   medium onion, chopped

4   (1-ounce) slices Canadian bacon, finely diced

1   tablespoon chopped garlic

$^1/_2$ teaspoon ground allspice

$^1/_2$ teaspoon ground cinnamon

$^1/_2$ teaspoon curry powder

1   cup long-grain brown rice

2   cups fat-free, low-sodium chicken broth (see note)

1   cup light coconut milk

2   cups cooked red beans or 1 (15-ounce) can, rinsed and drained

1   tablespoon chopped cilantro

1   tablespoon chopped scallions

In a 3- to 4-quart saucepan, heat the oil over medium-high heat. Add the onion and cook for 5 to 6 minutes, or until soft and just starting to brown. Add the bacon, garlic, allspice, cinnamon, and curry and cook for 2 minutes, or until fragrant. Add the rice and stir well.

Pour in the broth and coconut milk. Bring the mixture to a boil. Cover the pot, reduce the heat to a simmer, and cook until the rice is tender and has absorbed all the liquid. Stir in the beans. Allow to sit, covered, for 15 minutes before serving. Serve sprinkled with cilantro and scallions.

Note: For a soupier consistency, use an additional $^1/_2$ to 1 cup chicken broth.

Per serving: 210 calories, 5 g total fat (2 g saturated), 10 mg cholesterol, 220 mg sodium, 30 g total carbohydrates (1 g sugars), 6 g fiber, 10 g protein

BEANS 101

Bean varieties can be used interchangeably within reason; you might try black beans in a recipe that calls for red beans, or different sizes of white beans to find the flavor and consistency you like best. Experiment with beans in soups, salads, and side dishes; you'll create a variety of flavor sensations from a single recipe.

Serve these full-flavored beans with grilled chicken, or wrap them in a whole wheat tortilla with a drizzle of Salsa Vinaigrette (page 175) for a vegetarian burrito. The seasonings in this mouthwatering dish are versatile—you can substitute pinto or soybeans for the black beans, if you prefer.

TANGY BLACK BEANS

MAKES 8 (ABOUT $^2/_3$-CUP) SERVINGS

1   tablespoon olive oil

1   medium yellow onion, chopped

1   green bell pepper, diced

1   cup chopped tomatoes or 1 cup tomato sauce

1   tablespoon chopped garlic

1   bay leaf

1   teaspoon ground cumin

1   teaspoon chopped fresh oregano or $^1/_2$ teaspoon dried

1   teaspoon salt

$^1/_2$ teaspoon ground black pepper

$^1/_2$ teaspoon ground coriander

1   cup fat-free, low-sodium chicken broth or vegetable broth

3   cups cooked black beans or 2 (15.5-ounce) cans, rinsed and drained

1   tablespoon balsamic vinegar

1   tablespoon chopped cilantro (optional)

In a 3-quart saucepan, heat the oil over medium heat. Add the onion and bell pepper and cook for 5 minutes, or until soft.

Add the tomatoes or tomato sauce, garlic, bay leaf, cumin, oregano, salt, and black pepper and cook for about 3 minutes, or until the tomatoes are softened.

Carefully add the broth and beans. Reduce the heat to a simmer and cook for about 10 minutes.

Remove from the heat and stir in the vinegar. Serve hot, topped with cilantro, if desired.

Per serving: 120 calories, 2 g total fat (0 g saturated), 0 mg cholesterol, 75 mg sodium, 20 g total carbohydrates (3 g sugars), 6 g fiber, 6 g protein

This is a quick and easy side dish that can be prepared any time of year, though it's especially good in summer, when tomatoes are at their prime. Use a variety of tomatoes—yellow, green, or mottled heirloom—for a prettier presentation.

ASIAN TOMATOES AND RICE

MAKES 4 (¾-CUP) SERVINGS

2 cups cherry or grape tomatoes, halved

1⅓ cups steamed brown rice or 1 (180-gram) package steamed brown rice (I used Annie Chun's)

¼ cup Asian Salad Dressing (page 185)

1 tablespoon chopped cilantro

Combine the tomatoes, rice, dressing, and cilantro in a bowl and toss to combine.

Per serving: 171 calories, 1 g total fat (0 g saturated), 0 mg cholesterol, 430 mg sodium, 35 g total carbohydrates (2 g sugars), 2 g fiber, 4 g protein

THE GREAT CILANTRO DIVIDE

Also called Chinese or Mexican parsley, cilantro is an herb that most people tend to love or hate. While some people enjoy the hit of fresh, bright flavor it adds to many dishes, others pick up an unpleasant, soapy taste from cilantro. If you want to avoid using it, try substituting a combination of fresh chopped mint or basil with Italian parsley instead.

VEGETABLES

From crunchy to creamy, spicy to sweet—vegetables are the cornerstone of a healthy diet. Vegetables add a variety of flavors and textures to food and come in a luscious palette of colors that brighten our plates. With so many attractive qualities, vegetables should be high on our list of favorite foods. So why do they so often fall to the bottom of the pack?

According to data from the Centers for Disease Control and Prevention (CDC), in 2009 only 27.4 percent of Americans ate at least three servings of vegetables per day. And just 14 percent of Americans ate a full five servings (two fruits and three vegetables) of produce daily.

Misconceptions that vegetables are bland, expensive, and time-consuming to prepare all contribute to our national nutrition deficit. And the ready availability of so many prepackaged snack foods doesn't help, either. Eating an apple-flavored granola bar isn't the same thing as eating an apple. Even when a product label lists fruits and vegetables as ingredients, don't be fooled: They are no substitute for the real thing in terms of nutrition and often contain calorie-boosting fats and sugars to boot.

You may subscribe to the popular misconception that vegetables aren't filling, but nothing could be further from the truth. In fact, most vegetables have a high water content, so eating a substantial quantity delivers satisfying bulk with just a few calories. Vegetables are also loaded with fiber—which, in addition to making you feel full, also helps lower your risk of diabetes and heart disease.

I don't need to tell you that it's important to eat your vegetables. Aim to get a full 4 cups of them into your diet daily. To incorporate more vegetables into your diet, give the following strategies a try:

- **Consider frozen.** If fresh vegetables aren't available or are too pricey, it's fine to cook with frozen varieties; just opt for the versions without added salt or sugar.

- **Buy green wisely.** Certified Organic products must meet USDA federal standards of being grown without the use of most conventional pesticides or fertilizers, bioengineering, or radiation. In an ideal world, we'd all eat organic produce all the time, but since it tends to be more expensive than conventionally grown fruits and vegetables, limit organic purchases if need be to those thin-skinned fruits and vegetables especially prone to pesticide exposure—such as peaches and apricots, cherries and bell peppers, celery and spinach. For more information on organics, see the Shopping Sources section (page 199).

- **Think beyond carrots and celery.** There's no need to fall into a boring vegetable routine! Especially during the spring and summer, dozens of different

KEEPING IT FRESH

Vegetables and fruits spoil naturally over time as they age. Breaking or bruising them can also cause spoilage as bacteria are introduced into the flesh of the fruit. To keep your produce as fresh as possible:

- **Handle carefully.** Prevent breakage of skins and crushing of leaves as much as possible.
- **Remove damaged goods promptly.** If you spot a tomato with broken skin or outer leaves of lettuce that are mashed and slimy, discard them immediately and clean out the container to prevent spread of infection to other produce.
- **Use the produce drawer in the fridge.** Vegetables should not only be cool, but the air surrounding them should be slightly humid. By sealing them in a drawer, you help prevent moisture loss.
- **Ditch the plastic bags.** Not only is cutting your use of plastic bags environmentally friendly, but it's better for your veggies, too. Sealed plastic bags cut off the air supply and make them wilt faster; use paper bags instead, or simply wash and dry your produce and place it loose in the fridge drawer.
- **Don't spritz.** Although supermarkets mist their produce shelves, vegetables will get soggy and slimy if they're too wet. If you want to add moisture to the drawer, try covering them loosely with a damp (not dripping) paper towel.

---

vegetables are in season—try sampling a new veggie each week to discover your favorites.

- **Eat what you like.** This may sound like a no-brainer, but if you hate brussels sprouts, forcing yourself to eat them because they're "good for you" isn't going to warm you to the idea of vegetables. Discover the vegetables you enjoy and try out new recipes that incorporate them.

- **Fire them up.** As you'll find in the recipes that follow, roasting, pureeing, or grilling fresh vegetables unlocks new flavor profiles for even the most familiar of veggies. And adding a healthy dash of herbs and spices complements vegetable flavors, making for a rich taste experience.

- **Put vegetables in the spotlight.** We tend to think of vegetables as side dishes, but they make flavorful and filling entrées. Vegetables deserve a prime piece of real estate on our lunch and dinner plates—half of the plate. The other half is reserved for moderate portions of lean protein and whole grains.

HOW CLEAN ARE YOUR VEGGIES?

Raw vegetables are tasty in a salad—but are they safe? Recent reports about spinach and lettuce carrying *E. coli* or toxic chemicals may tempt you to buy one of the several products that claim to remove harmful pesticides and bacteria from your fruits and veggies. But these products are for the most part no more effective than rinsing in water. To ensure you're eating clean produce:

Soak vegetables in a bowl of water. This is an especially effective technique for spinach and lettuce with grit on the leaves, and also for leeks, which can have dirt lodged between their layers.

After soaking, spray with a homemade solution of 3 percent hydrogen peroxide (this is the type sold in drugstores as a disinfectant) followed by a spritz of vinegar. The substances will combine on the food and release germ-killing oxygen.

After spraying, wash vegetables vigorously under running water, carefully separating leaves to remove any remaining dirt from nooks and crannies.

If this process is too time-consuming for you, you can always skip ahead to the final step and just give your veggies a thorough rinse under running water. And to save time during meal prep, consider washing herbs and greens in advance; you can let them dry in a colander or use a salad spinner, and then rebag them for hassle-free use later.

Fennel is sometimes overlooked as an ingredient in hot dishes, because it's often served raw, in salads. But roasting fennel brings out a sweeter, more complex flavor. Here, the addition of roasted fennel adds big flavor to the simplest ingredients.

ROASTED FENNEL WITH LENTILS

MAKES 8 (½-CUP) SERVINGS

1 teaspoon canola or olive oil

1 medium yellow onion, chopped

½ cup chopped carrot

1 tablespoon chopped garlic

1 bay leaf

1 teaspoon chopped fresh thyme or ½ teaspoon dried

1 teaspoon ground mustard

1 cup brown lentils, rinsed and picked over

2–2½ cups fat-free, low-sodium chicken broth or vegetable broth

2 medium bulbs fennel, trimmed, quartered, cored, and cut crosswise into ¼-inch-thick slices

1 tablespoon olive oil

1 tablespoon balsamic vinegar

Salt and ground black pepper to taste

1 tablespoon chopped parsley, for garnish

Freshly grated Parmesan cheese, for garnish (optional)

Preheat the oven to 450°F.

In a 2-quart saucepan, heat the canola oil over medium-high heat. Add the onion and carrot and cook for 5 minutes, or until the vegetables are soft and just starting to brown.

Add the garlic and cook for 1 minute longer; do not let the garlic brown. Add the bay leaf, thyme, mustard, lentils, and 2 cups of the broth. Bring the mixture to a boil. Reduce the heat and simmer, partially covered, for about 20 minutes, or until the lentils are tender. Stir occasionally while simmering and add the remaining ½ cup broth if necessary.

While the lentils are simmering, combine the fennel and olive oil in a medium bowl and toss well. Spread evenly on a baking sheet and roast for about 15 minutes, stirring occasionally, until the fennel is cooked and just starting to brown. Remove from the oven and drizzle with the vinegar. Toss gently to coat.

Stir the roasted fennel into the cooked lentils. Season with salt and pepper. Transfer to a serving dish and garnish with the parsley and Parmesan, if desired.

Per serving: 130 calories, 3 g total fat (0 g saturated), 0 mg cholesterol, 150 mg sodium, 21 g total carbohydrates (2 g sugars), 8 g fiber, 8 g protein

Mushrooms add such meaty richness to this vegetable side dish. Feel free to substitute shiitakes or creminis for the portobellos, if you prefer. The earthiness of the vegetables goes especially nicely with grilled steak and a glass of red wine.

PORTOBELLOS AND ASPARAGUS

MAKES 4 (¹/₂-CUP) SERVINGS

2 teaspoons canola or olive oil

3 cups sliced portobello mushrooms (about 2 large portobellos, stems and black gills removed)

2 tablespoons chopped shallots

3 cups 1¹/₂-inch asparagus pieces, from about 1 pound (see note)

1 teaspoon low-sodium soy sauce

3 (¹/₂-ounce) slices nitrite-free turkey (or pork) bacon, cooked until crisp, drained well, and crumbled

1 tablespoon grated Parmigiano-Reggiano cheese

In a nonstick skillet, heat the oil over medium-high heat. Add the mushrooms and cook for about 3 minutes, or until they just start to soften and release their liquid. Add the shallots and cook for another minute.

Add the asparagus and cook for 3 minutes longer, or until the asparagus is just crisp-tender.

Drizzle the soy sauce over the veggies and sprinkle with the bacon crumbles and cheese. Toss well and serve hot.

Note: Instead of asparagus, you can substitute 1 (9-ounce) bag (12 cups) fresh spinach. Add to the mushrooms and cover for a few minutes until wilted. Stir well and add the remaining ingredients.

Per serving: 60 calories, 1 g total fat (<1 g saturated), 20 mg cholesterol, 110 mg sodium, 7 g total carbohydrates (2 g sugars), 2 g fiber, 6 g protein

THE MAGIC OF MUSHROOMS

Loaded with nutrients, mushrooms are also very high in water (which makes them filling). A great addition to salads and stir-fries, they're also delicious when stuffed and baked. Large mushrooms are excellent when grilled and make a great replacement for meat. When buying fresh mushrooms, make sure they are firm. Store them wrapped loosely in plastic in the refrigerator. Before use, wipe them with a damp paper towel or, if necessary, rinse them with cold water and dry thoroughly.

This Mediterranean-inspired dish can be served hot or cold. Add grilled chicken, fish, or shrimp for a delicious, satisfying meal. You can prepare this a day ahead of time: Cover, store in the fridge, and reheat before serving.

GREEK EGGPLANT WITH ROASTED TOMATO SAUCE AND FETA

MAKES 4 SERVINGS

2 teaspoons olive oil

½ medium onion, chopped

1 tablespoon minced garlic

1 (14.5-ounce) can no-salt-added fire-roasted diced tomatoes

¾ teaspoon dried oregano

⅛ teaspoon ground cinnamon

1 eggplant (about 1¼ pounds)

¼ cup crumbled low-fat feta cheese

8 kalamata or other black olives, pitted and sliced

2 teaspoons grated lemon zest

1 tablespoon flat-leaf (Italian) parsley, coarsely chopped

In a large nonstick skillet, heat the oil over medium-high heat. Add the onion and cook for about 5 minutes, or until soft and just starting to brown. Add the garlic and cook for 1 minute longer; do not let the garlic brown. Add the tomatoes, oregano, and cinnamon and simmer for about 4 minutes. Set aside.

Preheat the broiler. Slice the eggplant lengthwise into ¼-inch-thick slices. Lightly coat 2 baking sheets with cooking spray. Arrange the eggplant in a single layer on the sheets. Coat the eggplant lightly with cooking spray. Broil for about 8 minutes, or until tender and very lightly browned.

Layer half of the eggplant in a 2-quart serving dish (or an 8 × 8-inch pan). Top with half the tomato sauce. Repeat. Top with the cheese, olives, lemon zest, and parsley. Serve hot or at room temperature.

Per serving: 140 calories, 6 g total fat (2 g saturated), 5 mg cholesterol, 375 mg sodium, 18 g total carbohydrates (8 g sugars), 6 g fiber, 6 g protein

Sometimes rapini (broccoli rabe) can taste a little bitter. If your rapini is on the bitter side, drizzle it with a tablespoon or so of balsamic vinegar. This festive and colorful dish deserves a place on your holiday table.

RAPINI SAUTÉ

MAKES 8 (1-CUP) SERVINGS

2   tablespoons canola oil

3   bunches rapini (broccoli rabe), about 3¼ pounds, cut into 3-inch pieces

3   large cloves garlic, minced or crushed through a press

½   teaspoon salt

1½ cups peeled, diced roasted red bell pepper (see note, page 57)

3   tablespoons slivered almonds, toasted

Heat a very large Dutch oven or large skillet over medium-high heat. Add the oil to the pan. Add the rapini, garlic, and salt and toss well. Reduce the heat to medium-low, cover, and cook for 10 minutes, stirring occasionally, until the rapini is tender.

Add the roasted pepper and toasted almonds, toss, and serve.

Per serving: 110 calories, 5 g total fat (0 g saturated), 0 mg cholesterol, 55 mg sodium, 11 g total carbohydrates (3 g sugars), 1 g fiber, 7 g protein

BROCCOLI'S NUTRITIOUS COUSIN

Also known as broccoli rabe, rapini is a dark green, leafy vegetable with scattered clusters of broccoli-like buds. While we tend to eat only the large clusters of broccoli buds (not the stems or leaves), the whole rapini plant is edible, and its leaves are especially high in vitamin A.

Both broccoli and rapini are related to cabbage, and like cabbage, their sulfur-containing compounds can become pungent when cooked. In fact, the longer you cook these vegetables, the more odor molecules are produced—a good reason to eat them *al dente* after briefly boiling, roasting, or steaming them.

110 CALORIES

This pretty, rustic side dish dresses up any dinner table in minutes. The aromatic curry combined with the sweet flavor of acorn squash and the nuttiness of Parmesan make this an autumnal favorite.

ROASTED ACORN SQUASH WITH CURRY AND PARMESAN

MAKES 4 SERVINGS

1   medium acorn squash (1½ pounds)

2   teaspoons olive oil

¼   teaspoon Garlic Salt (page 193)

¼   teaspoon curry powder

1   tablespoon grated Parmigiano-Reggiano cheese

2   teaspoons chopped flat-leaf (Italian) parsley

Preheat the oven to 375°F. Lightly coat a rectangular baking dish with cooking spray.

Wash the squash and halve lengthwise (see note). Scrape out and discard the seeds. Cut each half crosswise into ½-inch-thick half-moons.

Combine the oil, Garlic Salt, and curry powder in a small bowl. Brush each squash slice with the oil mixture and arrange the half-moons in the baking dish with slight overlap.

Bake for 25 minutes, or until the squash is tender. Remove from the oven and sprinkle with the cheese and parsley. Serve immediately.

Note: For easier slicing, soften the whole unpeeled squash first by microwaving on high for 3 minutes. Cool and then slice as described.

Per serving: 90 calories, 4 g total fat (<1 g saturated), 0 mg cholesterol, 190 mg sodium, 14 g total carbohydrates (3 g sugars), 2 g fiber, 2 g protein

Braising is a basic cooking technique that infuses deep, rich flavors into vegetables or meat in a short amount of time. Underrated greens such as kale can simmer into a sumptuous pot of rich flavors with a few simple ingredients. This dish is the perfect accompaniment for roasted or grilled chicken.

BRAISED KALE WITH ONIONS AND ANCHOVIES

MAKES 6 ($\frac{2}{3}$-CUP) SERVINGS

Salt

1   pound kale (about 2 bunches), cleaned, ribs removed, and leaves cut crosswise into 1-inch slices

1   teaspoon canola oil

$\frac{1}{2}$ cup chopped yellow onion

4   oil-packed anchovies, finely chopped

$\frac{1}{2}$ cup fat-free, low-sodium chicken broth

2   teaspoons grated Parmigiano-Reggiano cheese

Bring a large pot of salted water to a boil. Add the kale and cook for 5 minutes, or until almost tender. Drain well.

In a large nonstick skillet, heat the oil over medium-low heat. Stir in the onion and anchovies and cook for about 5 minutes, stirring occasionally, until the onion has softened. Deglaze the pan with the broth, stirring up any browned bits from the bottom of the pan.

Reduce the heat to low and simmer for about 2 minutes. Add the blanched kale and simmer, covered, for about 8 minutes, or until the kale is very tender. If the kale is too dry, add a splash of broth and continue braising. Transfer the kale to a warmed serving bowl, sprinkle with the cheese, and serve hot.

Per serving: 120 calories, 4 g total fat (1 g saturated), 25 mg cholesterol, 880 mg sodium, 9 g total carbohydrates (0 g sugars), 2 g fiber, 12 g protein

FRUIT AND DESSERT

Ah, dessert. For those of us with a sweet tooth, the last course is when our willpower evaporates, sometimes transforming a healthy meal into a high-calorie splurge. From cheesecake to brownies to crème brûlée, there is no shortage of calorie-rich favorites that tempt us off the righteous path and into the sticky brambles of sugary excess. These temptations are usually full of sugar and fat but offer little in the way of nutritional value.

Not only does sugar offer few health benefits, but it can also contribute to a world of health problems, from tooth decay to diabetes. There's even evidence that sugar can boost triglyceride levels, increasing the risk of heart disease.

But there's no need to swear off sweets altogether. You don't need to sit through the last course of your meal clutching a cup of decaf and averting your eyes from your neighbors' treats. Think of dessert as an opportunity to reward yourself—with healthy choices.

There are plenty of ways to make those choices both decadent and delicious. But admittedly, if you've been eating a lot of sweets with added sugar, you may need to push the reset button on your palate. Not only do humans naturally crave sweet foods, but we also consume a lot more sugar than we're even aware of. Many packaged foods and beverages contain added sugar in order to boost flavor or texture, help preserve foods such as jams and jellies, or make baked goods rise. So even if you've been skipping dessert, you're probably eating more sugar than you think. Most Americans consume 22 teaspoons of added sugar daily. That's just shy of a half cup—yikes!

Instead of using refined sugar to create sweetness, the desserts on the pages that follow rely on a few simple guidelines.

ARTIFICIAL SWEETENERS: THE BOTTOM LINE

Artificial sweeteners are the subject of much controversy, despite numerous studies that have demonstrated that they're safe when consumed in moderation. But beyond toxicity concerns, artificial sweeteners are problematic for many people who are trying to lose weight, because while they lower the calorie counts of sweet snacks, they have also been linked to increased cravings for sugary foods. If you're trying to lose weight, a better strategy is to retrain your palate toward healthier, less-sweet choices.

Make fruit front and center. Cultivate an appreciation for the naturally sweet flavor of fresh fruit, and you'll reap ample rewards. A wide variety of succulent fruits can satisfy your sweet tooth while supplying vitamins, antioxidants, and fiber.

It's important to use perfectly ripe fruits when they're the star of your dish, but it can be hard to know when a piece of fruit is ready; some fruits continue to ripen after picking, and some don't. *Climacteric* fruits are often picked well before they ripen to better withstand transit, but they will continue to ripen after you've brought them home. *Nonclimacteric* fruits won't ripen once picked; what you see at the market is what you get.

You can speed the ripening of climacteric fruits by taking them out of the refrigerator; cool air slows the ripening process. If you're in a real hurry, you can place the unripe fruits loosely in a paper bag; the gases they emit while ripening will be trapped and speed the process further. Just a little gas goes a long way, though, so be sure to punch a couple of holes in the bag to let some of it escape—and check the progress every 12 hours or so to make sure you don't end up with overripe or spoiled fruit.

NONCLIMACTERIC FRUITS INCLUDE:

- Cherries
- Citrus fruits
- Cucumbers
- Grapes
- Pineapples
- Pomegranates
- Soft berries (e.g., blackberries, raspberries)
- Watermelon

CLIMACTERIC FRUITS INCLUDE:

- Apples
- Apricots
- Avocados
- Bananas
- Blueberries
- Figs
- Honeydew and cantaloupe melons
- Kiwifruit
- Mangoes
- Peaches and nectarines
- Pears
- Plums
- Tomatoes

Use natural sweeteners. There are many no- or low-calorie natural sweeteners available that can be used as healthy alternatives to sugar. See page 142 for a list of recommended sweeteners.

Spice it up. Spices like ginger, cinnamon, and cloves impart a hint of sweetness without added sugar.

Spotlight chocolate. Yes, chocolate! While chocolate in candy form—cocoa that's been combined with sugar and cocoa butter (and often milk fats, as well)—isn't a healthy choice, unsweetened cocoa powder is an antioxidant powerhouse. Ounce for ounce, cocoa powder contains the highest concentration of antioxidants compared to other foods, and its flavonoid content helps protect against heart disease and some cancers.

Start schooling your palate with these recipes, and soon you won't crave sweets the way you used to. You'll also have a new arsenal of techniques for creating your own decadent—and healthy—sweet treats.

NATURAL SWEETENERS: FIVE TO TRY

Instead of relying on white sugar to add sweetness to desserts, try these natural options. Unlike artificial sweeteners, most of these alternatives do contain some calories, but they are all-natural and offer some nutritive benefits, as well.

Agave nectar is extracted from the agave plant and is a little thinner than honey. Neutral in flavor, 1 teaspoon of agave nectar has 15 calories.

Honey contains antioxidants and can add floral notes as well as sweetness. The darker the honey, the higher the concentration of antioxidants. One teaspoon of honey has 21 calories.

Molasses is the dark-colored syrup that's left behind after sugar processing. It has relatively low sugar content and provides calcium, iron, magnesium, and potassium in addition to antioxidants. Blackstrap molasses is very intense in color and flavor—and explosively rich in antioxidants. One teaspoon of molasses has 16 calories.

Stevia is a natural no-calorie sweetener made from the leaf of a South American herb. It's much sweeter than sugar, so use sparingly. Take caution with stevia products that claim to be measurable (meaning one to one with sugar). They often contain bulking agents made of starches and simple carbs. One teaspoon of stevia has zero calories.

Xylitol occurs naturally in many fruits and vegetables, and for commercial production is extracted from hardwood trees and corncobs. A white powder, it has the same sweetness and bulk as sugar but one-third the calories. One teaspoon of xylitol has 10 calories.

This flan tastes like a rich, custardy version of pumpkin pie. If you have leftover pumpkin, try making a pumpkin smoothie with yogurt, milk, a few sweet spices like cinnamon, ginger, and cloves, and a drizzle of sweetener.

PUMPKIN FLAN

MAKES 8 FLANS

3	large eggs, preferably omega-3-enriched
1¼	cups unsweetened pumpkin puree
¼	cup + 3 tablespoons maple syrup
5½	teaspoons canola oil
1½	teaspoons vanilla extract
¾	teaspoon ground cinnamon
⅜	teaspoon ground ginger
¼	teaspoon ground cloves
¼	teaspoon salt
1½	cups 1% milk, heated until very hot
	Ground nutmeg, for garnish

Preheat the oven to 350°F with an oven rack in the center position. Coat eight 6-ounce custard cups with canola oil cooking spray and set them in a 13 × 9-inch baking pan.

In a large bowl, beat the eggs slightly with a small whisk. Add the pumpkin puree, maple syrup, oil, vanilla extract, cinnamon, ginger, cloves, and salt and beat until blended thoroughly. Mix in the hot milk until blended. There will be 4 cups of liquid. Pour ½ cup of the flan mixture into each of the custard cups.

Bring about 3 cups of water to a light simmer on top of the stove. Place the baking pan on the pulled-out oven rack and carefully pour the hot water into the baking pan until it comes up to the level of the custard inside the cups.

Bake for 40 to 45 minutes, or until just set around the edges but still a little loose in the center; the center will jiggle a little when shaken.

Carefully remove the pan from the oven. Remove the cups from the water bath with tongs and place on a rack to cool. Cover with plastic wrap and refrigerate for several hours. Serve cold, garnished with ground nutmeg.

Per flan: 190 calories, 7 g total fat (2 g saturated), 110 mg cholesterol, 220 mg sodium, 24 g total carbohydrates (18 g sugars), 2 g fiber, 6 g protein

PUMPKIN: IT'S NOT JUST FOR AUTUMN

When you think of pumpkin, jack-o'-lanterns and pumpkin pie may be the first things that come to mind, but there are many uses for this Native American vine fruit. The flesh is a rich source of antioxidants and beta-carotene and makes an excellent base for smoothies and desserts. Pumpkin seeds (pepitas) are a good source of omega-3 fatty acids and iron.

This sinful and irresistible (and gluten-free!) brownie is cakey, moist, and sweet. Dark cocoa powder and coconut add richness to the flavor. If you don't like coconut, you can use an equal amount of almond meal instead.

GERMAN CHOCOLATE BROWNIES

MAKES 25 BROWNIES

1 cup quinoa flour (see Shopping Sources/ Grains, Nuts, and Legumes, page 200)

²/₃ cup unsweetened shredded coconut

½ cup natural unsweetened cocoa powder

1 teaspoon baking powder

¼ teaspoon salt

1 cup agave nectar

¼ cup canola oil

2 large eggs, preferably omega-3-enriched

2 teaspoons vanilla extract

½ cup chopped toasted pecans

Preheat the oven to 325°F with an oven rack in the center position. Lightly coat an 8 × 8-inch baking pan with canola oil cooking spray.

Combine the quinoa flour, coconut, cocoa, baking powder, and salt in a medium bowl. Add the agave nectar, oil, eggs, and vanilla and stir just to combine. Stir in the nuts. There will be 2½ cups of batter. Pour the batter into the baking pan.

Bake for 25 to 30 minutes, or until a toothpick inserted in the center comes out barely clean. The brownies will just be starting to shrink from the sides of the pan. Do not overbake. Cool completely in the pan on a rack. Cut into 25 brownies.

Per brownie: 120 calories, 6 g total fat (2 g saturated), 15 mg cholesterol, 55 mg sodium, 16 g total carbohydrates (11 g sugars), 2 g fiber, 2 g protein

DON'T GO DUTCH WITH COCOA

Cocoa's abundant polyphenols are acidic, which means the antioxidant numbers are reduced when cocoa powder is alkalized. Alkali is sometimes added to cocoa during processing to create consistent color, flavor, and texture. This type of cocoa is labeled Dutch process. To ensure that you get a product with no added alkali—and the most antioxidants—choose "natural," not Dutch process.

These creamy custards highlight sweet spices and will satisfy your dessert cravings, dialing down the amount of sweetener required. Serve them warm for the taste of gingerbread straight from the oven, or cool for a refreshing treat.

OLD-FASHIONED GINGERSNAP CUSTARD

MAKES 4 (½-CUP) SERVINGS

  2   large eggs, preferably omega-3-enriched
 ¼   cup agave nectar
  1   teaspoon vanilla extract
 ½   teaspoon ground cinnamon
 ¼   teaspoon ground ginger
 ⅛   teaspoon ground cloves
 ⅛   teaspoon salt
1½   cups 1% milk, heated until very hot
       Ground nutmeg, for garnish (optional)

Preheat the oven to 350°F with an oven rack in the center position. Coat four 6-ounce custard cups with cooking spray and set them in a baking pan or dish large enough to hold them without crowding.

In a large bowl, beat the eggs slightly with a fork or small whisk. Add the agave nectar, vanilla extract, cinnamon, ginger, cloves, and salt and whisk to combine. Mix in the hot milk until blended. There will be about 2 cups. Pour ½ cup of custard mixture into each of the custard cups.

Bring about 3 cups water to a light simmer on top of the stove (you can use a teakettle for this). Place the baking pan on the pulled-out oven rack and carefully pour the hot water into the pan until it comes up to the level of the custard inside the cups.

Bake the custards for 30 to 35 minutes, or until set around the edges but still loose in the center. Carefully remove the pan from the oven. Remove the cups from the water bath with tongs and place on a rack. If serving the custards hot, allow them to cool for 10 minutes. If serving cold, let them cool, then cover with plastic wrap and refrigerate for several hours. Sprinkle nutmeg on the custard just before serving, if desired.

Per serving: 140 calories, 3 g total fat (1 g saturated), 110 mg cholesterol, 160 mg sodium, 42 g total carbohydrates (20 g sugars), 0 g fiber, 7 g protein

This recipe whips together in a snap if you have a chocolaty sweet tooth but only a couple of minutes to spare. It yields only a handful of truffles, because these are so addictive it's hard to eat just one—but you can easily scale up for a larger batch.

CHOCOLATE NUT TRUFFLES

MAKES 4 TRUFFLES

½ cup chopped dates

¼ cup chopped pistachios or toasted walnuts

1 tablespoon natural unsweetened cocoa powder + additional for rolling (optional)

½ teaspoon vanilla extract

1 teaspoon water (optional)

Combine the dates, nuts, and 1 tablespoon cocoa in a food processor. Pulse until finely chopped. Add the vanilla extract and pulse a few more times, until the mixture just pulls together. If the dates are very dry, add the water.

Transfer the mixture to a small bowl and shape into 4 "truffles" with a 2-tablespoon scoop. Roll in extra cocoa powder, if desired. Try to eat just one!

Per truffle: 110 calories, 5 g total fat (0 g saturated), 0 mg cholesterol, 0 mg sodium, 18 g total carbohydrates (14 g sugars), 2 g fiber, 3 g protein

A NUTTY FOUNTAIN OF YOUTH

Pistachios deliver protein, good fats, and dietary fiber, which can increase your feeling of satiety, or fullness. A 1-ounce serving of pistachios (about 49 kernels) contains 170 calories, a variety of beneficial vitamins and minerals, and 10 different anti-aging antioxidants.

These biscotti are a bit more delicate than some you may have made before; the combination of whole wheat flour and cornmeal creates a cookie that easily crumbles, so be gentle when slicing. Slivers of prunes or dried blueberries substitute nicely for the currants.

GINGER CURRANT BISCOTTI

MAKES ABOUT 36 BISCOTTI

½ cup agave nectar

⅓ cup canola oil

1 large egg, preferably omega-3-enriched

1 tablespoon vanilla extract

1 teaspoon grated lemon or orange zest

2¼ cups white whole wheat flour (I used King Arthur brand)

2 tablespoons stone-ground cornmeal

1 teaspoon baking powder

1 teaspoon ground ginger

¼ teaspoon salt

⅓ cup dried currants

¼ cup finely chopped crystallized ginger

¼ cup chopped pistachios or toasted walnuts

Preheat the oven to 350°F with an oven rack in the center position. Lightly coat a 15 × 10-inch baking sheet with cooking spray.

In a medium bowl, whisk together the agave nectar, oil, egg, vanilla extract, and lemon zest. Combine the flour, cornmeal, baking powder, ginger, and salt in a large bowl. Make a well in the center of the flour mixture and pour in the agave mixture. Stir just to combine. Stir in the currants, crystallized ginger, and nuts. The dough will be soft.

Transfer the dough to a work surface. Form into 2 logs about 10 inches long and 1½ inches in diameter. Flatten the logs with the palm of your hand to a 1-inch thickness. Place on the baking sheet and bake for 15 minutes. Transfer to a rack to cool for 10 minutes.

While the biscotti logs are still warm, carefully slice each of them diagonally with a serrated knife into about eighteen ½-inch slices.

Place the biscotti, cut sides down, on an ungreased 15 × 10-inch baking sheet and return to the oven to bake for 15 minutes, or until light golden brown. Transfer to racks to cool completely.

Per biscotti: 80 calories, 3 g total fat (0 g saturated), 5 mg cholesterol, 20 mg sodium, 12 g total carbohydrates (5 g sugars), 1 g fiber, 1 g protein

Not really a cake, a crisp, or a cobbler, this luscious dessert is spicy, sweet, and, quite simply, irresistible. For true decadence, serve warm with a dollop of fat-free vanilla frozen yogurt or Greek yogurt.

MAPLE-NUT APPLE TREAT

MAKES 12 SERVINGS

FILLING

- **6** crisp sweet-tart apples, such as Fuji, peeled, cored, quartered lengthwise, and cut crosswise into $1/2$-inch-thick slices
- **1** tablespoon lemon juice
- **1** teaspoon vanilla extract

TOPPING

- $1/3$ cup old-fashioned rolled oats
- $1/3$ cup white whole wheat flour (I used King Arthur brand)
- **2** tablespoons chopped walnuts or pistachios
- **2** teaspoons ground cinnamon
- $1/2$ teaspoon baking powder
- $1/2$ teaspoon ground ginger
- $1/4$ teaspoon baking soda
- $1/4$ teaspoon ground allspice
- $1/4$ teaspoon ground cloves
- $1/4$ teaspoon salt
- $1/8$ teaspoon ground nutmeg
- $1/3$ cup buttermilk
- $1/3$ cup maple syrup
- $1/4$ cup canola oil
- **1** teaspoon vanilla extract

Preheat the oven to 375°F with an oven rack in the center position. Lightly coat a 9 × 9-inch baking pan with cooking spray.

To make the filling: In a large bowl, toss the apples with the lemon juice and vanilla extract. Transfer to the baking dish.

To make the topping: Combine the oats, flour, nuts, cinnamon, baking powder, ginger, baking soda, allspice, cloves, salt, and nutmeg in a medium bowl. Mix well. Combine the buttermilk, maple syrup, oil, and vanilla extract in a small bowl. Quickly fold the buttermilk mixture into the dry ingredients. Spoon the topping over the apples. It will just cover the apples.

Bake for 30 minutes, or until the topping is puffed. Spoon into bowls and serve warm.

Per serving: 190 calories, 6 g total fat (0 g saturated), 0 mg cholesterol, 105 mg sodium, 35 g total carbohydrates (23 g sugars), 4 g fiber, 2 g protein

I almost put this recipe at the beginning of the book, in the breakfast chapter, but I decided its scrumptious factor just screamed dessert. The banana yogurt is fabulous by itself, or as the base for a gorgeous fruit plate of kiwi, melon, and berries. Here it's simply layered with fresh berries and crunchy granola.

BANANA YOGURT PARFAITS

MAKES 2 SERVINGS

1 cup fat-free plain Greek yogurt

1 very ripe medium banana, diced

½ teaspoon vanilla extract

½ cup fresh berries (any combination of blueberries, raspberries, sliced strawberries, etc.)

½ cup low-fat granola

1 tablespoon finely shredded fresh mint, for garnish

Place the yogurt, banana, and vanilla extract in a food processor and combine until pureed.

Spoon about 5 tablespoons of the banana yogurt into each of 2 parfait glasses or dessert bowls. Top each with 2 tablespoons of berries and 2 tablespoons of granola. Repeat the layers of yogurt, berries, and granola. Top the parfaits with fresh mint. Serve immediately.

Per serving: 160 calories, <1 g total fat (0 g saturated), 0 mg cholesterol, 55 mg sodium, 29 g total carbohydrates (16 g sugars), 6 g fiber, 14 g protein

Not overly sweet, the richness of cocoa and toasted nuts shines through in this elegant companion to tea or coffee.

FUDGE PECAN TEA COOKIES
MAKES 3 DOZEN SMALL COOKIES

1 cup whole wheat pastry flour

⅓ cup natural unsweetened cocoa powder

½ cup pecans, lightly toasted and chopped

½ teaspoon baking powder

⅛ teaspoon salt

6 tablespoons maple syrup or agave nectar

2 tablespoons unsweetened vanilla almond milk (see Shopping Sources/ Nondairy Milk, page 203)

1 large egg, preferably omega-3-enriched

1 teaspoon vanilla extract

Preheat the oven to 325°F. Lightly coat 2 baking sheets with cooking spray.

Combine the flour, cocoa, pecans, baking powder, and salt in a medium bowl. Whisk together the maple syrup or agave nectar, egg, and vanilla extract in a small bowl. Pour the wet ingredients into the flour mixture and stir just to combine.

Halve the dough and form each half into a 9-inch log about 1½ inches in diameter. Wrap in plastic wrap and refrigerate for at least 1 hour or up to 1 day.

Remove the plastic wrap. Cut each log into 18 slices about ½ inch thick and place on the prepared baking sheets. (Be sure to use a very sharp slicing knife. If you're having difficulty, you can also pop the dough into the freezer for about 30 minutes to facilitate easier slicing.)

Bake for 20 minutes, switching the positions of the pans once midway. Cool on the baking sheets on a rack for 10 minutes. When completely cool, store in an airtight container.

Per cookie: 30 calories, 2 g total fat (0 g saturated), 5 mg cholesterol, 10 mg sodium, 5 g total carbohydrates (2 g sugars), 1 g fiber, 1 g protein

BEVERAGES

When we're trying to eat healthier and lose weight, most of us focus on improving the quality of the food on our plates. But what we consume from cans, bottles, mugs, wineglasses, and to-go cups has just as much of an impact on our waistlines.

The truth is, most of the bottled and canned drinks on the market are pitfalls for anyone looking to control his or her calorie intake. And few of them provide any true health benefits, though many claim to. Just a few of the dangers that lurk in your glass:

Sugar water. Most of us know by now that sodas are packed with sugar, but so are supposedly "healthier" options such as fruit juices, iced teas (including many green teas), and enhanced water beverages that offer vitamins and other healthy-sounding benefits.

Overhyped sports drinks. Unless you're exercising at high intensity for more than 1 hour, you don't need to replace electrolytes, carbs, and potassium using sports drinks; you'll get enough of these nutrients in the course of your regular meals, and you don't need the extra calories these drinks contain. Instead, drink plenty of water, and if you need a recovery boost, consider a protein-rich drink such as the Very Berry Smoothie on page 165.

The morning drive-thru. The good news is that coffee contains natural antioxidants that may protect against cancer and type 2 diabetes—so drinking it in moderation is perfectly acceptable. But we run into trouble when we enhance our morning joe with whole milk, half-and-half, sugar, cream, "shots" of sweet flavorings, syrups, and whipped cream. Many morning beverages can contain more calories than your dinner.

Just one more drink . . . Wine is antioxidant-rich, and studies suggest that moderate intake (a single 5-ounce glass with dinner) may reduce risk of developing heart disease and diabetes. But in general, alcohol is high in calories—and its intoxicating effects limit your inhibitions, making it harder to say no not only to another drink, but also to the high-calorie snacks that always seem to accompany festive times (from Buffalo wings to cheese and crackers).

The list above may seem to take all the fun out of your glass—but don't be fooled. There are plenty of fresh, flavorful beverage options that not only quench your thirst but contribute nutritional benefits as well. The refreshing recipes in this chapter are low in calories and were created based on these healthy drinking principles:

Pep up water to get your fill. By now, you probably know that you should be drinking plenty of water every day—eight to twelve 8-ounce glasses, or more if you're exercising. Water is something of a miracle elixir; proper hydration improves all your bodily functions at the cellular level, from your heart

THE INS AND OUTS OF FIZZ

When you want a break from plain water, carbonated varieties can add a pleasant change with no additional calories. Just be sure to choose wisely and avoid blends that contain added juice and sugar.

- **Mineral water,** as the name suggests, contains minerals and sometimes gases and is sourced from wells or springs. It's naturally effervescent and low-calorie.

- **Club soda,** also called soda water or seltzer water, is water injected with carbon dioxide to create fizz.

- **Tonic water** Is charged with carbon dioxide and flavored with fruit extracts, sugar, and small amounts of bitter quinine. Because of the flavorings, it has about 80 calories per serving and is high in carbohydrates.

to your energy level. And water can contribute to a feeling of fullness, so downing a glass before you start each meal can not only help you make your 8- to 12-glass quota, but can also help you eat less.

Flavor with whole fruits, not fruit juice. Sliced fruit can impart a sweet or tangy flavor without adding the refined sugar many fruit juices contain. Try experimenting with different fruits and even vegetable and herb flavorings. Sliced cucumber or a few torn mint or basil leaves with lemon can make a glass of plain water extra refreshing.

Think tea. Hot or iced, unsweetened tea is a zero-calorie beverage that offers a lot of nutritional benefits. Green tea is an especially good choice; its caffeine is surrounded by tannic acid compounds that slow its release into the bloodstream, minimizing jittery effects. Green tea is a good source of the antioxidant EGCG, which has a mild metabolism-boosting effect. Four cups of green tea per day can kick up your metabolism by 80 calories. Its rich antioxidant reserves are also thought to help combat diseases from Alzheimer's to cancer.

Drink plenty of calcium. It's important to keep your bones supplied with the calcium you need to stay strong—1,000 milligrams daily or, for women over 50, 1,200 milligrams daily. And since caffeine can hinder calcium absorption, you need to consume even more calcium if you are a heavy coffee drinker. Whether in the form of milk, yogurt, or kefir, use beverages that boost your calcium intake throughout the day.

This pungent extract offers an easy way to get an antioxidant fix between meals. For a supercharged sipper, replace the sparkling water with iced green tea. And for a health-conscious cocktail, try mixing 2 tablespoons of ginger syrup with 1 ounce of dark rum. Top with a splash of sparkling water and serve over ice with a lime wedge.

AMBER GINGER ALE

MAKES 3 CUPS SYRUP, OR 12 (10-OUNCE) DRINKS

GINGER SYRUP

- 3 cups water
- 8 ounces unpeeled fresh ginger, grated in a food processor
- ½ cup agave nectar
- 2 tablespoons lime juice
- 2 tablespoons vanilla extract

GINGER ALE

- Ginger Syrup (above)
- 2 quarts chilled sparkling water
- Ice cubes

To make the syrup: In a 1½-quart saucepan, bring the water and ginger to a rapid boil over medium-high heat. Boil for 5 minutes. Remove from the heat and let steep for 20 minutes. Strain the syrup through a fine sieve and pour into a 1-quart jar. Stir in the agave nectar, lime juice, and vanilla extract. Let cool. Store the syrup in the refrigerator for up to 3 weeks.

To make ginger ale: To make a pitcherful, combine the syrup and sparkling water in a 2½- to 3-quart pitcher. Add ice and stir. For a single serving, add ¼ cup ginger syrup to 8 ounces sparkling water.

Per drink: 50 calories, 0 g total fat (0 g saturated), 0 mg cholesterol, 0 mg sodium, 12 g total carbohydrates (11 g sugars), 0 g fiber, 0 g protein

Like yogurt, kefir is a fermented dairy product—but unlike yogurt, kefir is fermented with a greater variety of bacteria and yeast, resulting in a higher concentration of probiotics to help aid digestion. This protein-rich shake makes for a great breakfast on the go.

KIWI KEFIR SHAKE

MAKES 2 (¾-CUP) SERVINGS

1 cup low-fat plain kefir (see Shopping Sources/Other Beverages, page 203)

1 medium kiwifruit, peeled and sliced

2 teaspoons almond butter

½ teaspoon vanilla extract

½ very ripe medium banana, frozen and cut into 1-inch pieces

Combine the kefir, kiwi, almond butter, vanilla extract, and banana in a blender and puree until smooth. Serve immediately.

Per serving: 170 calories, 5 g total fat (1 g saturated), 5 mg cholesterol, 95 mg sodium, 29 g total carbohydrates (19 g sugars), 3 g fiber, 6 g protein

WHAT IS KEFIR?

Kefir, which originated in the Middle East, was traditionally made with camel's milk. Today it is commercially produced using cow's milk. The fermentation process gives it a tangy, yogurtlike taste and a texture that's both smooth and slightly fizzy. Kefir is sold in low-fat and fat-free varieties in cartons or bottles and should be kept refrigerated.

Nut or seed milks are made by soaking nuts or seeds in water, blending them, and then straining the liquid. Almond milk in particular has recently become a popular dairy- and soy-free alternative for smoothies and cereal. When preparing this shake, be sure the almond milk and yogurt are ice cold and the banana is frozen to ensure a thick, creamy texture.

FROSTY DATE SHAKE

MAKES 2 (1-CUP) SERVINGS

1/4   cup (2 ounces) pitted dates (see note)

1   cup unsweetened vanilla almond milk (see Shopping Sources/Nondairy Milk, page 203)

1/2   cup fat-free plain Greek yogurt

1   very ripe banana, frozen and cut into 1-inch chunks

4   ice cubes

1/2   teaspoon vanilla extract

1/8   teaspoon ground nutmeg + additional for garnish

Combine the dates, almond milk, yogurt, banana, ice, vanilla extract, and 1/8 teaspoon nutmeg in a blender and blend until smooth and frothy, about 30 seconds. Pour into a tall, chilled glass and garnish with a dusting of nutmeg.

Note: If the dates are hard, place them in a small bowl and sprinkle with warm water. Let soften for 5 minutes, then drain off excess water.

Per serving: 100 calories, 2 g total fat (0 g saturated), 0 mg cholesterol, 110 mg sodium, 17 g total carbohydrates (11 g sugars), 2 g fiber, 6 g protein

---

DRIED FRUITS PACK A PUNCH

Since dried fruits contain less water than fresh fruits, their flavor and calories are much more concentrated. That means a little goes a long way. Dried fruits such as currants, dates, prunes, and apricots are a great way to add texture and a burst of flavor to baked goods, but use them in moderation and be mindful of your portion sizes.

You can mix and match your favorite berries in this smoothie to create a number of different flavors and textures. If fresh berries aren't available, use frozen berries—just eliminate the added ice.

VERY BERRY SMOOTHIE
MAKES 2 (1-CUP) SERVINGS

1   cup low-fat plain kefir (see Shopping Sources/Other Beverages, page 203)

½   cup blackberries

½   cup blueberries

½   teaspoon vanilla extract

    Pinch of ground cloves

6   ice cubes

Combine the kefir, berries, vanilla extract, cloves, and ice in a blender and puree until smooth. Serve immediately.

Per serving: 90 calories, 2 g total fat (1 g saturated), 5 mg cholesterol, 70 mg sodium, 15 g total carbohydrates (11 g sugars), 3 g fiber, 6 g protein

WHAT'S IN THAT SMOOTHIE?

Smoothies can be a healthy way to start off your morning—but beware: Many varieties offered at popular smoothie chains are little more than fruity milkshakes. For example, a Jamba Juice Orange Dream Machine contains orange juice, orange sherbet—and no actual oranges! But at the same smoothie shop, you can also order a Five Fruit Frenzy, made with strawberries, blueberries, bananas, mangoes, and peaches—a much healthier option. Read labels carefully before you order your morning smoothie, or better yet, save calories and money by blending your own drink at home!

Any melon can be substituted for the watermelon, and any soft fruit or berry can replace the strawberries, so feel free to tailor this recipe to your liking. This pretty drink makes a nice base for a cocktail, too—just add 1 ounce of vodka or rum.

SPARKLING AGUA FRESCA

MAKES 6 (1-CUP) SERVINGS

6 cups seedless watermelon cubes

1 cup strawberries, halved

1 tablespoon lime juice

1 tablespoon minced fresh ginger

2 cups chilled water or sparkling water
Fresh mint or basil leaves, for garnish

Combine the watermelon, strawberries, lime juice, and ginger in a blender or food processor and puree until smooth. Strain. There will be about 4 cups.

Pour into a heavy glass pitcher, cover with plastic wrap, and chill for at least 2 hours. Just before serving, stir in the chilled water. Garnish with mint or basil leaves.

Note: The agua fresca will keep for 2 to 3 days in the refrigerator.

Per serving: 50 calories, 0 g total fat (0 g saturated), 0 mg cholesterol, 5 mg sodium, 17 g total carbohydrates (15 g sugars), 1 g fiber, 1 g protein

The fragrance of *masala chai* is as intoxicating as its complex flavor. Traditionally prepared by steeping spices in hot water and milk before adding black tea, this rendition uses almond milk. It is soothing and restorative and takes just minutes to prepare. This spicy chai is equally delicious served piping hot in a mug or chilled over ice for a refreshing treat.

BLACK ALMOND CHAI

MAKES 6 (1-CUP) SERVINGS

4 cups water

6 (¼-inch-thick) slices peeled fresh ginger

1 (3-inch) cinnamon stick

6 whole cloves

½ teaspoon ground cardamom

6 black tea bags

2 cups unsweetened vanilla almond milk (see Shopping Sources/Nondairy Milk, page 203)

3 tablespoons agave nectar or dark honey

In a saucepan, combine the water, ginger, cinnamon, cloves, and cardamom. Bring to a boil over medium heat, then reduce the heat and simmer for about 3 minutes. Remove from the heat. Add the tea bags and steep in the spice mixture for 5 minutes. Strain into a container and discard the solids.

Return the tea concentrate to the saucepan and add the almond milk. Simmer over low heat but do not boil. Whisk in the agave.

Note: You can double or even triple the amounts for the tea concentrate and store it in a sealed container in the refrigerator for up to 1 week. To prepare a single serving, mix ½ cup hot tea concentrate with ⅓ cup hot almond milk. Sweeten with 1½ teaspoons agave nectar or honey.

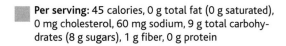 **Per serving:** 45 calories, 0 g total fat (0 g saturated), 0 mg cholesterol, 60 mg sodium, 9 g total carbohydrates (8 g sugars), 1 g fiber, 0 g protein

CLEAVE CLOVES WITH CAUTION

Intensely aromatic cloves are a popular spice for both sweet and savory dishes, and are available powdered or whole. If you grind your own cloves, though, be careful—the phenol chemicals in the spice have mildly corrosive properties and may pit or soften plastic parts of a grinder—embedding the strong scent of cloves in the appliance. Grind cloves with a stone mortar and pestle, or skip the process entirely and buy ground cloves.

CONDIMENTS AND SAUCES

They're quick. They're easy. They deliver big flavor in small doses and add the richness we crave to a variety of dishes. What's not to love about condiments?

Defined as relishes, sauces, dressings, or other food accompaniments, condiments can be used in a variety of ways to add zip and zest to a meal. You can use condiments in marinades and rubs before cooking, incorporate them into dishes as you cook, or offer them on the side at the table to give your guests control over the amount of flavor they want to add to their dish.

Types of condiments include:

Relishes, salsas, and chutneys. Incorporating chopped vegetables and fruits along with herbs and acidic liquids like vinegar or lemon juice, these accompaniments can be chunky or smooth. Although generally paired with savory dishes, they can have sweet overtones, and range from mild to spicy.

Fruit butters, jellies, jams, and preserves. Fruit or fruit juice, sugar, water, and sometimes pectin are the traditional ingredients in these spreads; to make them more nutritious, reduce the amount of sweetener to bring out intense fruit flavors, and use a healthy alternative to white sugar, such as agave nectar. Or if you're buying them, look for sugar-free, 100 percent fruit varieties.

Dressings. Sauces that are used to top salads and other dishes served cold or at room temperature, dressings can range far beyond the standard oil and vinegar combination. Using aromatic combinations of herbs, flavorful vinegars or citrus juices, and minimal fat can make dressings healthy as well as delicious.

Sauces. Any thickened, flavored liquid that accompanies food qualifies as a sauce—from a savory tomato sauce for pasta to a sweet raspberry sauce for cakes. Swap rich staples like hollandaise sauce for healthier alternatives that use fruits, vegetables, herbs, and spices to deliver flavor and texture. To achieve richness with less fat and calories, try substituting avocado for mayo.

Glazes. A thin coating of intense sweet or savory flavor can add another layer of zest to a dish without adding fat. Reductions of meat stocks or broths, melted dark chocolate, or fruit spread can all be used in sparing amounts to boost flavor without sacrificing health.

Marinades. As described in The Essentials of Healthy Flavor (page 2), marinades bathe meat, fish, and vegetables in an aromatic liquid prior to cooking. A marinade typically consists of an acidic substance, like lemon juice or red wine, plus spices and herbs.

The great news is that most condiments are a snap to make—and you can whip up large batches so you have plenty on hand to amp up the flavor of a quick weeknight meal. Most of the condiments in the recipes that follow will keep in the refrigerator for a couple of weeks, giving you plenty of time to try them with a variety of dishes.

To maximize a condiment's flavor, consider how the taste and texture will interact with the ingredients of the dish it accompanies. Often, contrasting sensations enhance overall flavor. For example, a smooth fruit butter can add richness to the crunch of a whole wheat English muffin; a spicy salsa adds zest to the rich, buttery texture of a plump halibut fillet.

To get you started, I've suggested pairings for the condiments that follow with other recipes throughout the book—but once you've tried them, you'll soon be able to improvise your own flavor combinations to create new favorites.

CONDIMENT MUST-HAVES IN MY PANTRY

In addition to the recipes in this chapter, here is a list of bottled condiments I always have on hand for a quick fix or to pull together a last-minute appetizer or meal:

Barbecue sauce

Capers

Catsup (ketchup)

Chutney

Harissa

Horseradish

Hot sauce

Jam (all fruit spreads)

Mustards—whole grain, Dijon, and honey

Salsa

Soy sauce

Tapenade

Vinegars—balsamic, cider, white wine, red wine, and malt

Worcestershire sauce

This rich-tasting dressing contains no oil, so it's low in calories but very high in flavor. It takes just minutes to make and is a perfect accompaniment to grilled fish, Spicy Beef Satays (page 63), or Salade Niçoise (page 73).

CREAMY MUSTARD DRESSING

MAKES 1¼ CUPS

1	cup soft silken tofu, drained
2	tablespoons Dijon mustard
1	tablespoon lemon juice
1	tablespoon capers
1	tablespoon chopped shallots
1½	teaspoons Worcestershire sauce
½	teaspoon smoked salt (optional)
⅛	teaspoon ground black pepper

Combine the tofu, mustard, lemon juice, capers, shallots, Worcestershire sauce, smoked salt (if desired), and pepper in a blender or food processor and puree until smooth. For a thinner dressing, add 2 tablespoons water. The dressing can be stored in the refrigerator for up to 2 weeks.

Per **2 tablespoons:** 15 calories, <1 g total fat (0 g saturated), 0 mg cholesterol, 75 mg sodium, 1 g total carbohydrates (0 g sugars), 0 g fiber, 1 g protein

TOFU: LOW-CALORIE AND NUTRIENT-DENSE

Tofu, also called soybean curd or bean curd, is made from curdled soymilk, which is dried and pressed in a process similar to making cheese. Its bland, slightly nutty flavor makes it a versatile ingredient in main dishes and condiments alike. It also packs a nutrient punch, delivering 260 milligrams of calcium, 12 grams of protein, and 2 milligrams of iron in a ½ cup serving, which contains less than 100 calories.

This vinaigrette is delicious in a chopped salad, poured over a simple grilled chicken breast, or tossed with legumes and whole grains, such as Tangy Black Beans (page 120).

SALSA VINAIGRETTE

MAKES ABOUT 1 CUP

1 cup roasted tomato salsa (or your favorite jarred salsa)

¼ cup lime juice or cider vinegar

3 tablespoons canola or olive oil

¼ teaspoon ground black pepper

½ teaspoon Chipotle Puree (page 192; optional)

Combine the ingredients in a blender or food processor and puree until smooth. The vinaigrette will keep in the refrigerator for up to 2 weeks.

Per tablespoon: 25 calories, 3 g total fat (0 g saturated), 0 mg cholesterol, 0 mg sodium, 1 g total carbohydrates (0 g sugars), 0 g fiber, 0 g protein

This zippy cocktail sauce doesn't contain any sugar, unlike most bottled brands. If you prefer a milder flavor, omit the horseradish. It's the perfect dip with fresh seafood, such as the grilled shrimp cocktail (page 54).

FIRE-ROASTED COCKTAIL SAUCE

MAKES ABOUT 1 CUP

1 cup canned no-salt-added fire-roasted diced tomatoes

1 tablespoon horseradish

1 tablespoon lime juice

¼ teaspoon Chipotle Puree (page 192; optional)

Combine the ingredients in a blender or food processor and puree until smooth. Transfer to a jar and chill for at least 30 minutes. The sauce will keep in the refrigerator for about 1 month.

Per ¼ cup: 20 calories, 0 g total fat (0 g saturated), 0 mg cholesterol, 160 mg sodium, 4 g total carbohydrates (2 g sugars), <1 g fiber, 1 g protein

Sofrito is a sautéed vegetable mixture used as a seasoning in much of Latin America and the Caribbean. There are as many variations of sofrito as there are curries or moles, though it usually contains bell pepper, cilantro, garlic, onion, and sometimes tomatoes. Sofrito is typically chunky, but I've pureed it to use as a sauce. Sofrito is delicious on eggs, such as Huevos Sofrito (page 43), and is the perfect topping for enchiladas and Southwestern-style pasta.

EASY SOFRITO SAUCE

MAKES 2 CUPS

1 red bell pepper, roasted (see note, page 57) and peeled

½ cup chopped onion

½ cup canned no-salt-added fire-roasted diced tomatoes

½ cup fat-free, low-sodium chicken or vegetable broth

¼ cup packed cilantro sprigs

2 teaspoons minced garlic

1 teaspoon chopped fresh oregano or ½ teaspoon dried

½ teaspoon ground cumin

½ teaspoon smoked paprika

½ teaspoon Chipotle Puree (page 192; optional)

Salt and ground black pepper to taste

Combine the roasted pepper, onion, tomatoes, broth, cilantro, garlic, oregano, cumin, smoked paprika, and Chipotle Puree, if desired, in a blender or food processor and puree until smooth.

Transfer the mixture to a skillet and simmer, stirring, for 3 minutes, or until the vegetables are softened and the mixture is fragrant. Season with salt and black pepper. Use immediately, freeze, or refrigerate for 3 or 4 days.

Per ½ cup: 30 calories, 0 g total fat (0 g saturated), 0 mg cholesterol, 130 mg sodium, 6 g total carbohydrates (3 g sugars), 1 g fiber, 1 g protein

There's a real surprise ingredient in this addictive condiment—bananas! This sweet-spicy barbecue sauce is truly finger-licking good and is delicious with Beer-Braised Pork Tacos (page 94) or on any sandwich.

SPICY CARIBBEAN BARBECUE SAUCE

MAKES 6 CUPS

1½   pounds ripe bananas (about 5 medium)

2   cups water

1   (14.5-ounce) can no-salt-added fire-roasted diced tomatoes

1   medium red bell pepper, roasted (see note, page 57), peeled, and coarsely chopped

⅔   cup apple cider vinegar

½   cup chopped onion

½   cup chopped prunes

1   teaspoon chopped garlic

1   teaspoon ground allspice

½   teaspoon chili powder

½   teaspoon ground cinnamon

½   teaspoon ground nutmeg

¼   teaspoon ground black pepper

¼   teaspoon ground cloves

2   teaspoons Chipotle Puree (page 192)

1   teaspoon smoked salt (optional)

Combine the bananas, water, tomatoes, roasted pepper, vinegar, onion, prunes, garlic, allspice, chili powder, cinnamon, nutmeg, black pepper, and cloves in a blender or food processor and puree until smooth.

Transfer the mixture to a 3- or 4-quart saucepan and bring to a boil. Reduce the heat and simmer, partially covered, over low heat for 30 minutes. Stir in the Chipotle Puree and smoked salt, if desired. There will be about 6 cups of sauce. Transfer to jars and refrigerate. The sauce will keep in the refrigerator for about 2 weeks. Extra sauce may also be frozen in 1-cup containers.

Per ¼ cup: 40 calories, 0 g total fat (0 g saturated), 0 mg cholesterol, 40 mg sodium, 10 g total carbohydrates (6 g sugars), 1 g fiber, 1 g protein

BANANAS: A STARCHY TREAT

If you're trying to cut carbs, consume bananas sparingly, as they're rich in carbohydrates. In Africa, Central and South America, and Asia, where they're grown, bananas' high carbohydrate count makes them an important food staple. Half the world's crop is cooked and consumed as a starchy vegetable much like a potato, using either unripe bananas or nonsweetening varieties collectively known as plantains. In the United States, it's more common to consume bananas ripe, when the starch has converted to sugar. A medium banana supplies more than 500 milligrams of potassium, which helps the body excrete excess sodium and boosts muscle power—making this fruit a good postexercise recovery snack.

This "mayo" is a delicious way to enjoy a creamy, rich spread on your sandwich while using only good fats and a fraction of the calories of mayonnaise. It is also a perfect accompaniment to sashimi or small rice crackers; or try using a dollop in place of sliced avocado in the Tortilla Soup with Avocados (page 79).

ASIAN AVO "MAYO"

MAKES ¾ CUP

1	ripe Hass avocado, coarsely chopped
3	tablespoons warm water
2½	teaspoons rice vinegar
2	teaspoons chopped pickled sushi ginger
1	teaspoon low-sodium soy sauce
1	teaspoon Dijon mustard
½	teaspoon toasted sesame oil

Combine the avocado, water, vinegar, ginger, soy sauce, mustard, and oil in a food processor or blender and puree until smooth. Transfer to a small jar and refrigerate. The "mayo" keeps refrigerated for 2 days.

Per tablespoon: 25 calories, 2 g total fat (0 g saturated), 0 mg cholesterol, 10 mg sodium, 1 g total carbohydrates (0 g sugars), 0 g fiber, 0 g protein

THE PERFECT AVOCADO

Avocados ripen and spoil quickly, so if you buy them ripe, be sure to use them immediately. You can also buy them slightly immature and keep them refrigerated until a day or two before you need them, at which time you should store them at room temperature to finish the ripening process. To hasten ripening, place avocados in a brown bag with an apple. The natural ethylene gas released by the apple hastens the ripening process.

This vinaigrette tastes indulgent. Thanks to a dollop of Greek yogurt, it has a creamy, luscious texture. It is a delicious dressing for salads like the Shredded Beets with Crumbled Feta (page 76) or drizzled on grilled fish or chicken. Try substituting other combinations of citrus fruits, such as lemons, grapefruit, or blood oranges, to create unique flavors.

CITRUS VINAIGRETTE

MAKES 1 CUP

½ cup fat-free plain Greek yogurt

1 teaspoon grated lime zest

¼ cup lime juice

2 tablespoons chopped cilantro leaves

1 tablespoon agave nectar or honey

1 tablespoon unseasoned rice vinegar

1 teaspoon chopped garlic

¼ cup canola or light olive oil

Salt and ground black pepper to taste

Combine the yogurt, lime zest and juice, cilantro, agave nectar or honey, vinegar, and garlic in a food processor and puree until smooth. While the machine is running, slowly drizzle in the oil until incorporated. Season with salt and pepper. The dressing will keep in the refrigerator for about 2 weeks.

Per tablespoon: 40 calories, 3 g total fat (0 g saturated), 0 mg cholesterol, 0 mg sodium, 2 g total carbohydrates (1 g sugars), 0 g fiber, 1 g protein

CITRUS APPEAL

If you're juicing citrus fruit and don't have immediate need for the zest, remove it with a vegetable peeler and set it out on a plate to dry. Once it's completely dry, store it in a jar so that you'll always have zest on hand even when you're out of fresh citrus fruit.

The stunning color of this versatile, sweet sauce adds instant dazzle to any plate. It is gorgeous spread over sorbet, drizzled onto a fruit plate, stirred into yogurt, or layered in Banana Yogurt Parfaits (page 154).

BLACKBERRY ORANGE SAUCE

MAKES 1½ CUPS

- 2 tablespoons agave nectar or dark honey
- 2 tablespoons Grand Marnier (optional)
- 2 tablespoons torn fresh mint leaves
- 2 cups fresh blackberries or 1 (16-ounce) bag frozen unsweetened blackberries, thawed
- 1 tablespoon grated or crumbled dried orange zest

In a small, heavy, nonreactive saucepan, combine the agave nectar, Grand Marnier, if desired, and mint leaves. Bring to a simmer over low heat and cook just until the mixture is hot, but not boiling. Remove from the heat and let cool.

Place the berries in a food processor or blender. Add the cooled syrup and orange zest. Process until smooth. For a silky-smooth sauce (but a lower yield with less fiber), pass through a very fine strainer. The sauce keeps refrigerated for 2 to 3 days.

Per ¼ cup: 50 calories, 0 g total fat (0 g saturated), 0 mg cholesterol, 0 mg sodium, 10 g total carbohydrates (8 g sugars), 3 g fiber, 1 g protein

This is an easy way to make rich-tasting gravy without relying on cholesterol-laden pan drippings. It's a delicious accompaniment to any protein, from poultry such as the Turkey Roulade (page 96) to pork loin. Feel free to substitute dried mushrooms such as shiitakes or morels.

PORCINI MUSHROOM GRAVY

MAKES 2 CUPS

½ ounce dried porcini mushrooms (see Shopping Sources/General Specialty Foods, page 200)

2 tablespoons warm water

1½ tablespoons canola oil

6 tablespoons white whole wheat flour (I used King Arthur brand)

2 cups fat-free, low-sodium chicken broth

1 teaspoon onion powder

¾ teaspoon salt (optional)

¼ teaspoon ground black pepper (or to taste)

Soften the mushrooms in the warm water for 5 minutes.

Meanwhile, in a 2-quart saucepan, heat the oil over medium heat. Whisk in the flour until blended and continue stirring until the roux is lightly browned and develops a nutty aroma, 2 to 3 minutes.

Whisk in the broth, onion powder, and salt, if desired. Bring to a gentle boil, stirring, and cook until just thickened. Cook and stir for 1 minute to remove the flour's raw starchy flavor. Remove from the heat and season with the pepper. Add the softened mushrooms and any soaking liquid.

Scrape the mixture into a food processor or food mill and puree. Return the mixture to the saucepan. Heat just to a simmer and serve hot.

Per ¼ cup: 50 calories, 3 g total fat (0 g saturated), 0 mg cholesterol, 115 mg sodium, 5 g total carbohydrates (0 g sugars), 2 g fiber, 1 g protein

This simple salad dressing takes just minutes to make and lends itself to a variety of uses, from sliced tomatoes to cabbage salad to side dishes like Asian Tomatoes and Rice (page 121).

ASIAN SALAD DRESSING

MAKES 1 CUP

¼ cup yellow or white miso

¼ cup rice vinegar

1 tablespoon low-sodium soy sauce

1 tablespoon Dijon mustard

1 tablespoon pickled sushi ginger

1 tablespoon toasted (or untoasted) sesame oil

1 tablespoon chopped shallots or garlic

1 tablespoon water

Combine the miso, vinegar, soy sauce, mustard, ginger, oil, shallots or garlic, and water in a food processor or blender and puree until smooth. Transfer to a jar and refrigerate. The dressing will keep for 2 weeks.

Per tablespoon: 15 calories, 1 g total fat (0 g saturated), 0 mg cholesterol, 150 mg sodium, 2 g total carbohydrates (1 g sugars), 0 g fiber, 0 g protein

Originally designed as an alternative to high-sugar cranberry sauce for a holiday meal, this chutney-like sauce is a delicious and traditional accompaniment to Turkey Roulade (page 96) but also makes a great topping for oatmeal or yogurt or spooned onto virtually anything when a sweet craving strikes.

WARM APPLE AND CRANBERRY SAUCE

MAKES 2$\frac{2}{3}$ CUPS

1 tablespoon canola oil

4 large Fuji apples (about 2 pounds), cored, quartered lengthwise, and cut crosswise into $\frac{1}{2}$-inch pieces

$\frac{1}{4}$ cup water

1 tablespoon lemon juice

$\frac{1}{4}$ cup coarsely chopped dried cranberries

$\frac{1}{2}$ teaspoon vanilla extract

$\frac{1}{4}$ teaspoon ground cinnamon

$\frac{1}{8}$ teaspoon salt (optional)

In a large heavy saucepan, heat the oil over medium heat. Add the apples and cook for about 10 minutes, or until the apples are lightly caramelized. Add the water and lemon juice and stir briefly to deglaze the pan.

Carefully transfer the hot apples to a food processor and pulse just a few times to a chunky consistency. Stir in the cranberries, vanilla extract, cinnamon, and salt, if desired. Serve warm.

Per $\frac{1}{3}$ cup: 40 calories, 1 g total fat (0 g saturated), 0 mg cholesterol, 0 mg sodium, 9 g total carbohydrates (6 g sugars), 2 g fiber, 0 g protein

PUCKER UP FOR VITAMIN C

Notoriously sour because of their high level of acid and very low sugar content, cranberries are loaded with vitamin C. You can buy them fresh, frozen, canned, or dried. Canned cranberries may contain added sugar, so when fresh ones aren't available, opt for frozen. Dried cranberries also make a great addition to trail mixes, salads, and hot cereal. When purchasing dried cranberries, be sure to choose those that are sweetened with fruit juice rather than sugar.

SALTS AND SEASONINGS

By now you know that fresh herbs and spices are a powerful tool in your flavor arsenal, especially when layered into a dish throughout the cooking process—from marinade to condiments to garnish.

In recent years, food marketers have recognized the value of these tasty, fat-free, low-calorie flavor helpers and have unleashed a variety of new products on the market—from flavored salts to varying combinations of spices, such as barbecue rubs and Italian seasoning mixes.

But with minimal effort, you can create your own unique seasoning blends, which not only saves you money but also allows you to customize your flavor agents and control sodium content.

There are many ways to create your own signature spice blends. The following techniques will allow you to have instant flavor at the ready in your pantry.

- **Rubs.** These mixtures coat the surface of food prior to cooking—adding a flavor kick with few calories and no fat.
- **Flavored salts.** Salt that has been infused with another layer of flavor does double duty for the amount of sodium added to the recipe.
- **Herb blends.** Created from mixtures of your favorite dried herbs, they're simple to make and give you easy access to the flavors you love for sauces and meals.
- **Purees and pastes.** Blending up a batch of pureed chile peppers or olives to dab onto dishes later is another timesaver, as well as a way to pinch pennies at the supermarket.

Because the flavor of chipotle chile peppers is so intense (and hot!), a teaspoon or a tablespoon is often all I need to impart the smokiness and heat I crave. Add a little of this puree to barbecue sauce, salsa, eggs, guacamole, or Fire-Roasted Chili (page 89).

CHIPOTLE PUREE

MAKES 1 CUP

1   (7-ounce) can chipotle chile peppers in adobo sauce (see note)

¼   cup water

Puree the contents of the can and the water in a blender or food processor until smooth. Transfer to a glass jar and store in the refrigerator. The puree keeps refrigerated for 1 month or more.

Note: Chipotle chile peppers are ripe jalapeño peppers that have been smoked. They are packed in a spicy sauce called adobo and sold in cans. They're available in Latin food markets, specialty foods stores, and some supermarkets.

Per teaspoon: 2 calories, 0 g total fat (0 g saturated), 0 mg cholesterol, 37 mg sodium, 1 g total carbohydrates (0 g sugars), 0 g fiber, 0 g protein

Store-purchased garlic salt can't compare with the flavor of this fresh version. It's delicious sprinkled on so many things and is a primary ingredient in other seasonings and rubs, such as Southwestern Mustard Rub (page 194). Because this recipe requires some time to prepare, I like to make a large batch. It also makes a great gift packaged in a pretty bottle with a homemade label.

GARLIC SALT

MAKES 1½ CUPS

1⅓ cups coarse sea salt

⅔ cup garlic cloves, peeled but whole

Preheat the oven to 170°F. Line a baking sheet with parchment paper.

Pour the salt into a food processor. With the machine running, add the garlic cloves through the feed tube and process until the mixture is transformed into a paste, scraping down the sides as necessary.

Transfer the garlic paste to the parchment-lined pan and spread out somewhat. Cover with a sheet of plastic wrap cut to the same size as the baking pan. Using a rolling pin, try to flatten the paste to a thin, even layer. Remove the plastic.

Place the garlic paste in the oven and leave it there for about 1 hour 30 minutes. The goal is to dry the paste but not cook it, which would change the flavor. You may turn off the oven and leave the garlic in overnight to be sure the paste is dry enough.

Return the completely dried paste to a food processor and process to a uniformly fine consistency. Store in an airtight container at room temperature.

Per teaspoon: 0 calories, 0 g total fat (0 g saturated), 0 mg cholesterol, 1,680 mg sodium, 0 g total carbohydrates (0 g sugars), 0 g fiber, 0 g protein

The advantage of a wet rub is that it really sticks to your food. If cooking meat, lightly scoring it first will help the flavors penetrate. Be sure to apply the rub at least 15 minutes before cooking and up to several hours before, depending on how thick the meat is and how robust the rub flavor is. Leftover rub keeps refrigerated for about 2 weeks. This blend is delicious on grilled pork tenderloin when served with Roasted Acorn Squash with Curry and Parmesan (page 135).

SOUTHWESTERN MUSTARD RUB

MAKES 1¼ CUPS, ENOUGH FOR 4 RUBS

1 cup Dijon mustard

½ cup finely chopped cilantro

¼ cup crumbled dried lime zest (see note)

1 tablespoon chili powder

1 tablespoon ground cumin

1 tablespoon Garlic Salt (page 193)

1 teaspoon ground black pepper

½ teaspoon dried oregano

Place the mustard, cilantro, lime zest, chili powder, cumin, Garlic Salt, pepper, and oregano in a blender or food processor and combine until smooth. Store in an airtight container in the refrigerator.

Note: Dried orange, lemon, or lime zest can be made simply at home. Using a vegetable peeler, remove the zest only (the colored outer layer) and not the white pith underneath. Spread on a plate to dry for several days until brittle. Store in an airtight container.

Per rub (5 tablespoons): 80 calories, 0 g total fat (0 g saturated), 0 mg cholesterol, 1,760 mg sodium, 15 g total carbohydrates (0 g sugars), 2 g fiber, 1 g protein

MEDICINAL MUSTARD

Mustard seeds and mustard greens contain potent antioxidants that fight the cellular damage caused by free radicals. Mustard also contains sulfur compounds with antibacterial, antiviral, and antifungal properties.

Two of my favorite things to roast are chicken and root vegetables. I season them both with rosemary and decided to make my own rosemary salt for that purpose. It's easy to make, is inexpensive, and adds incredible flavor to any dish, such as Grilled Root Vegetable Salad with Bacon and Chives (page 80).

ROSEMARY SALT

MAKES 2½ CUPS

2 cups coarse sea salt

1 cup coarsely chopped fresh rosemary

Place the salt and rosemary in a food processor. Process for about 30 seconds, or until well combined. Pulse a few more times if necessary, but don't overprocess, because you want to have a little bit of texture. Store in one or more airtight containers.

Per teaspoon: 0 calories, 0 g total fat (0 g saturated), 0 mg cholesterol, 1,450 mg sodium, 0 g total carbohydrates (0 g sugars), 0 g fiber, 0 g protein

REFERENCES

CHAPTER 1

American Heart Association. "What Is the 'Mediterranean' Diet?" http://www.americanheart.org/presenter.jhtml?identifier=4644 (accessed May 2010).

———. "Cholesterol." http://www.americanheart.org/presenter.jhtml?identifier=1516 (accessed May 2010).

———. "Know Your Fats." http://www.americanheart.org/presenter.jhtml?identifier=532 (accessed May 2010).

———. "Risk Factors and Coronary Heart Disease." http://www.americanheart.org/presenter.jhtml?identifier=4726 (accessed May 2010).

BBC. "Spices Recipes and Information." http://www.bbc.co.uk/food/spice (accessed May 2010).

Charley, Helen. *Food Science.* Englewood Cliffs, NJ: Merrill/Prentice Hall, 1982

Forberg, Cheryl. *Positively Ageless: A 28-Day Plan for a Younger, Slimmer, Sexier You.* New York: Rodale, 2008.

Forberg, Cheryl, Melissa Roberson, and *The Biggest Loser* Experts and Cast. *The Biggest Loser: Simple Swaps: 100 Easy Changes to Start Living a Healthier Lifestyle.* New York: Rodale, 2009.

GourmetSleuth.com. "Culinary Salt." http://www.gourmetsleuth.com/Articles/Exotic-Herbs-Spices-and-Salts-639/culinary-salt-guide.aspx (accessed May 2010).

Harvard School of Public Health. "The Nutrition Source: Fats and Cholesterol." http://www.hsph.harvard.edu/nutritionsource/what-should-you-eat/fats-and-cholesterol/ (accessed May 2010).

Herbst, Sharon Tyler. *The New Food Lover's Companion,* 2nd ed. Hauppauge, NY: Barron's Educational Series, 1995.

International Association for the Study of Obesity. "Global Prevalence of Adult Obesity," February 2010. http://www.iotf.org/database/documents/GlobalPrevalenceofAdultObesity10thFebruary2010.pdf (accessed May 2010).

Kasabian, David, and Anna Kasabian. *The Fifth Taste: Cooking with Umami, with Recipes from 25 of America's Best Chefs.* New York: Universe Publishing, 2005.

Le, C.N. "Asian Cuisine & Foods." From "Asian-Nation: The Landscape of Asian America." http://www.asian-nation.org/asian-food.shtml (accessed May 2010).

Mayoclinic.com. "Apple cider vinegar for weight loss: Effective?" from "Expert Answers." http://www.mayoclinic.com/health/apple-cider-vinegar-for-weight-loss/AN01816 (accessed May 2010).

McGee, Harold. *On Food and Cooking: The Science and Lore of the Kitchen.* New York: Collier Books, 1984.

Moskin, Julia. "Yes, MSG, the Secret Behind the Savor." *New York Times,* March 5, 2008. http://www.nytimes.com/2008/03/05/dining/05glute.html?_r=1 (accessed August 2010).

Reuters News Service. "Americans Eat Too Much Salt, CDC Says." March 26, 2009. http://www.reuters.com/article/idUSTRE52P65820090326 (accessed May 2010).

Subramanian, Sushma. "Fact or Fiction: Raw veggies are healthier than cooked ones." *Scientific American,* March 31, 2009. http://www.scientificamerican.com/article.cfm?id=raw-veggies-are-healthier (accessed May 2010).

"A Thumbnail History of Mexican Food," from "Mexican Mercados." http://www.mexicanmercados.com/food/foodhist.htm (accessed May 2010).

US Department of Health and Human Services. "Your Guide to Lowering Your Blood Pressure with DASH" (NIH Publication No. 06-4082), 2006. http://www.nhlbi.nih.gov/health/public/heart/hbp/dash/new_dash.pdf (accessed August 2010).

US National Institutes of Health. National Cancer Institute. "Heterocyclic Amines in Cooked Meats." http://www.cancer.gov/cancertopics/factsheet/Risk/heterocyclic-amines (accessed May 2010).

———. National Heart Lung and Blood Institute. "Your Guide to Lowering Your Cholesterol with TLC." http://www.nhlbi.nih.gov/health/public/heart/chol/chol_tlc.pdf (accessed May 2010).

———. "Reduce Salt and Sodium in Your Diet," from "Your Guide to Lowering High Blood Pressure." http://www.nhlbi.nih.gov/hbp/prevent/sodium/sodium.htm (accessed May 2010).

———. National Library of Medicine. Medline Plus. "Antioxidants." http://www.nlm.nih.gov/medlineplus/antioxidants.html (accessed May 2010).

Wolke, Robert L. *What Einstein Told His Cook 2: Further Adventures in Kitchen Science, The Sequel.* New York: W.W. Norton & Co., 2005.

CHAPTER 2: BREAKFAST

Herbst, Sharon Tyler. *The New Food Lover's Companion,* 2nd ed. Hauppauge, N.Y.: Barron's Educational Series, 1995.

Smith, A.P. "Stress, Breakfast Cereal Consumption and Cortisol," *Nutritional Neuroscience* 5, no. 2 (April 2002): 141–4.

US Department of Agriculture. Food Safety and Inspection Service. "Egg Products Preparation: Shell Eggs from Farm to Table." http://www.fsis.usda.gov/factsheets/Focus_On_Shell_Eggs/index.asp (accessed June 2010).

CHAPTER 3: APPETIZERS AND SNACKS

Bhaşan, Gillie, and Jonathan Bhaşan. *Classical Turkish Cooking.* New York: St. Martin's Press, 1997.

Herbst, Sharon Tyler. *The New Food Lover's Companion,* 2nd ed. Hauppauge, NY: Barron's Educational Series, 1995.

MayoClinic.com. "Dietary Fats: Know Which Types to Choose." http://www.mayoclinic.com/health/fat/NU00262 (accessed June 2010).

CHAPTER 4: SOUPS AND SALADS

Herbst, Sharon Tyler. *The New Food Lover's Companion,* 2nd ed. Hauppauge, NY: Barron's Educational Series, 1995.

McGee, Harold. *On Food and Cooking: The Science and Lore of the Kitchen.* New York: Collier Books, 1984.

CHAPTER 5: MEAT, FISH, AND POULTRY

Herbst, Sharon Tyler. *The New Food Lover's Companion,* 2nd ed. Hauppauge, NY: Barron's Educational Series, 1995.

CHAPTER 6: GRAINS AND LEGUMES

Harvard University Health Services. Nutrition Service. "Iron Content of Common Foods." http://huhs.harvard.edu/assets/File/OurServices/Service_Nutrition_Iron.pdf (accessed May 2010).

Herbst, Sharon Tyler. *The New Food Lover's Companion,* 2nd ed. Hauppauge, NY: Barron's Educational Series, 1995.

McGee, Harold. *On Food and Cooking: The Science and Lore of the Kitchen.* New York: Collier Books, 1984.

US Department of Health and Human Services. Centers for Disease Control and Prevention. "Fruit and Vegetable of the Month: Vegetable of the Month: Beans." http://www.fruitsandveggiesmatter.gov/month/beans.html (accessed May 2010).

US Dry Bean Council. "Beans for Health: Nutrient Profile of Beans." http://www.usdrybeans.com/library/Nutrient%20Profile.pdf (accessed May 2010).

US National Institutes of Health. National Library of Medicine. Medline Plus. "Protein in Diet." http://www.nlm.nih.gov/medlineplus/ency/article/002467.htm (accessed May 2010).

Wolke, Robert L. *What Einstein Told His Cook 2: Further Adventures in Kitchen Science, The Sequel.* New York: W.W. Norton & Co., 2005.

CHAPTER 7: VEGETABLES

Herbst, Sharon Tyler. *The New Food Lover's Companion,* 2nd ed. Hauppauge, NY: Barron's Educational Series, 1995.

MayoClinic.com. "Nutrition and Healthy Eating: Dietary Fiber: Essential for a Healthy Diet." http://www.mayoclinic.com/health/fiber/NU00033 (accessed June 2010).

McGee, Harold. *On Food and Cooking: The Science and Lore of the Kitchen.* New York: Collier Books, 1984.

US Department of Health and Human Services. Centers for Disease Control and Prevention. "Research: State Indicator Report on Fruits and Vegetables, 2009." http://www.fruitsandveggiesmatter.gov/health_professionals/statereport.html (accessed May 2010).

Wolke, Robert L. *What Einstein Told His Cook 2: Further Adventures in Kitchen Science, The Sequel.* New York: W.W. Norton & Co., 2005.

CHAPTER 8: FRUIT AND DESSERT

Forberg, Cheryl. *Positively Ageless: A 28-Day Plan for a Younger, Slimmer, Sexier You.* New York: Rodale, 2008.

MayoClinic.com. "Nutrition and Healthy Eating: Added Sugar: Don't Get Sabotaged by Sweeteners." http://www.mayoclinic.com/health/added-sugar/MY00845 (accessed May 2010).

———. "Nutrition and Healthy Eating: Artificial Sweeteners: Understanding These and Other Sugar Substitutes." http://www.mayoclinic.com/health/artificial-sweeteners/MY00073 (accessed May 2010).

McGee, Harold. *On Food and Cooking: The Science and Lore of the Kitchen*. New York: Collier Books, 1984.

Wolke, Robert L. *What Einstein Told His Cook 2: Further Adventures in Kitchen Science, The Sequel*. New York: W.W. Norton & Co., 2005.

CHAPTER 9: BEVERAGES

Herbst, Sharon Tyler. *The New Food Lover's Companion*, 2nd ed. Hauppauge, NY: Barron's Educational Series, 1995.

CHAPTER 10: CONDIMENTS AND SAUCES

Herbst, Sharon Tyler. *The New Food Lover's Companion*, 2nd ed. Hauppauge, N.Y.: Barron's Educational Series, 1995.

McGee, Harold. *On Food and Cooking: The Science and Lore of the Kitchen*. New York: Collier Books, 1984.

CHAPTER 11: SALTS AND SEASONINGS

No sources cited.

Flavor First Seasoning Blends in select sweet and savory flavor profiles are available for purchase at www.flavorfirst.com.

The listings below provide options for sourcing many of the ingredients called for in this book. Happily, most of these items are more widely available and easier to find than ever before. If you can't find something at the grocery store, always check out your local health food stores, ethnic food shops, and farmers' markets, as well.

FRUITS AND VEGETABLES

Community Supported Agriculture (CSA)

Community Supported Agriculture, or CSA, programs put you directly in touch with local farmers by providing a regular (weekly, biweekly, or monthly) allotment of fresh seasonal produce from their fields, which you can either pick up yourself or, with some CSAs, opt to have delivered to your home. CSAs are growing in popularity and can be an economical way to buy produce. If a weekly box contains too much food for you to use, consider splitting the loot with a friend or two. For more information, try:

- **www.nal.usda.gov/afsic/pubs/csa/csa.shtml**
  This USDA site includes helpful links to CSA listings and local farm finders.

- **localharvest.org/csa** Helpful tips for would-be CSA members, including how to select a program and a searchable database of local CSAs.

Farmers' Markets

The number of farmers' markets has tripled in the past 15 years. They're a great source of locally grown, fresh produce—and a fun way to learn about growers in your area. To find a market near you, search:

- **apps.ams.usda.gov/farmersmarkets** The USDA's searchable directory of farmers' markets now includes more than 6,000 listings.

- **localharvest.org** A searchable database of local farmers' markets also includes listings for grocery stores that supply organic produce, and information about CSAs.

- **farmersmarketcoalition.org** This site for market managers and workers includes state-by-state resource listings.

Melissa's/World Variety Produce, Inc.
P.O. Box 21127
Los Angeles, CA 90021
800-588-0151
www.melissas.com
In addition to selling fresh organic and exotic fruits and vegetables, Melissa's supplies dried mushrooms and other dried produce, herbs, organic agave nectar, whole grains, organic food products, and nuts. The Web site offers direct online ordering.

GENERAL SPECIALTY FOODS

Dean & DeLuca
Customer Care
4115 E. Harry
Wichita, KS 67218
800-221-7714
www.deandeluca.com
New York–based specialty purveyor offers chocolate, chipotle chiles, crystallized ginger, other spices, oils, tahini, sorghum syrup, teas, and coffees. The Web site offers direct online ordering as well as a listing of retail outlets.

eFoodPantry.com
P.O. Box 3483
Springfield, IL 62708
866-372-6879
www.efoodpantry.com
Sugar-free/diabetic products, gluten-free products, and organic pantry items such as unsweetened cocoa powder and preserves. The Web site offers direct online ordering.

iGourmet.com
508 Delaware Avenue
West Pittston, PA 18643
877-446-8763
www.igourmet.com
Oils, herbs, teas, unsweetened cocoa powder, fresh and dried produce (including dried mushrooms), nuts, and cheeses. The Web site offers direct online ordering.

Kalustyan's
123 Lexington Avenue
New York, NY 10016
212-685-3451 or 800-352-3451
www.kalustyans.com
Fine foods merchant offers spices, teas, tahini, legumes, sauces, salts, and more. The Web site offers direct online ordering.

GRAINS, NUTS, AND LEGUMES

Annie Chun's
P.O. Box 2418
San Rafael, CA 94912
866-595-8917
www.anniechun.com
Quick multigrain rice, black rice, and Asian sauces. The Web site includes a listing of retail stores where products are sold as well as direct online ordering.

Arrowhead Mills
The Hain Celestial Group, Inc.
4600 Sleepytime Drive
Boulder, CO 80301
800-434-4246
www.arrowheadmills.com
Whole grain flours, cornmeal, vital wheat gluten, gluten-free products, and nut butters. The Web site includes a listing of retail stores where products are sold as well as direct online ordering (click "Contact Us" to access both).

Bob's Red Mill Natural Foods
5000 SE International Way
Milwaukie, OR 97222
800-349-2173
www.bobsredmill.com
Whole grain flours, quinoa flour, vital wheat gluten, gluten-free products, seeds, beans, and bulk grains. The Web site includes a listing of retail stores where products are sold as well as direct online ordering.

Food for Life

P.O. Box 1434
Corona, CA 92878
800-797-5090
www.foodforlife.com
Sprouted organic whole grain breads and cereals, gluten-free products, and low-GI products. The Web site includes a listing of retail stores where products are sold.

Hodgson Mill

1100 Stevens Avenue
Effingham, IL 62401
800-347-0105
www.hodgsonmill.com
Whole wheat pastas, whole grain baking mixes, flaxseed products, soy products, gluten-free products. The Web site includes a listing of retail stores where products are sold as well as direct online ordering.

King Arthur Flour

58 Billings Farm Road
White River Junction, VT 05001
800-827-6836
www.kingarthurflour.com
Whole grain and nut flours, gluten-free products, baking mixes, chocolate, and spices. The Web site includes a listing of retail stores where products are sold as well as direct online ordering.

Living Tree Community Foods

P.O. Box 10082
Berkeley, CA 94709
800-260-5534
www.livingtreecommunity.com
Nuts, nut butters, oils, agave nectar, honey, flaxseed. The Web site offers direct online ordering.

The Nut Factory

P.O. Box 815
Greenacres, WA 99016
888-239-5288
www.thenutfactory.com
Nuts in their shells—including walnuts, almonds, filberts, and Brazil nuts. The Web site offers direct online ordering.

Nuts Online

125 Moen Street
Cranford, NJ 07016
800-558-6887
www.nutsonline.com
Nuts in their shells—including walnuts, almonds, filberts, Brazil nuts, pecans, pistachios, and peanuts—along with flaxseed and other seeds, dried fruits, teas, and nut butters. The Web site offers direct online ordering.

Quinoa Corporation

P.O. Box 279
Gardena, CA 90248
310-217-8125
www.quinoa.net
Boxed quinoa, quinoa flour, quinoa pastas, and ready-made precooked polenta. The Web site offers direct online ordering for large quantities (a case or more); or try amazon.com to order smaller amounts.

Rancho Gordo

1924 Yajome Street
Napa, CA 94559
707-259-1935
www.ranchogordo.com
Supplier of organic heirloom beans and other legumes, chiles and other spices, herbs, and quinoa. The Web site includes a listing of retail stores where products are sold as well as direct online ordering.

RiceSelect

1925 FM 2917
Alvin, TX 77511
800-993-7423
www.riceselect.com
Whole grain orzo and couscous, and brown and wild rice mixes. The Web site offers direct online ordering.

Sun Organic Farm

411 S. Las Posas Road
San Marcos, CA 92078
888-269-9888
www.sunorganic.com
Organic grains, flours, beans and other legumes, flaxseed, nuts and nut butters, seeds, oils, and dried vegetables. The Web site offers direct online ordering.

HERBS AND SPICES

Penzeys Spices
12001 W. Capitol Drive
Wauwatosa, WI 53222
800-741-7787
www.penzeys.com
A comprehensive catalog of herbs, spices, and seasonings, including sumac, crystallized ginger, and a variety of curry powders, along with unsweetened natural cocoa powders. The Web site offers direct online ordering as well as a listing of retail outlets.

The Spice House
1941 Central Street
Evanston, IL 60201
847-328-3711
www.thespicehouse.com
This Chicago-area merchant offers a comprehensive catalog of herbs and spices, including sumac, crystallized ginger, and a variety of curry powders. The Web site offers direct online ordering as well as a listing of retail outlets.

MEAT, POULTRY, AND FISH

Alaskan Harvest
8040 SE Stark Street
Portland, OR 97215
800-824-6389
www.alaskanharvest.com
Sustainably harvested wild ivory king salmon; king, silver, and sockeye salmon; and Alaskan black cod available year-round. The Web site offers direct online ordering.

Lobel's
1501 East Avenue, Suite 210
Rochester, NY 14610
877-783-4512
www.lobels.com
New York City–based butcher shop offers nationwide delivery of top-quality beef, lamb, pork, and poultry. The Web site offers direct online ordering.

Organic Prairie
CROPP Cooperative
One Organic Way
La Farge, WI 54639
888-444-6455
www.organicprairie.coop
Organic beef, pork, poultry, and sausages. The Web site offers direct online ordering.

Vital Choice Seafood
P.O. Box 4121
Bellingham, WA 98227
800-608-4825
www.vitalchoice.com
Sustainably harvested wild salmon, sablefish, scallops, tuna, and more. The Web site offers direct online ordering.

Wild Planet
1585 Heartwood Drive, Suite F
McKinleyville, CA 95519
800-998-9946
www.wildplanetfoods.com
Sustainable canned shrimp, tuna, salmon, and sardines. The Web site offers direct online ordering.

Wise Organic Pastures
685 Myrtle Avenue
Brooklyn, NY 11205
718-596-0400
www.wiseorganicpastures.com
Organic and kosher chicken, turkey, and beef from a family farm in Pennsylvania. The Web site offers direct online ordering.

SWEETENERS

Barry Farm Foods
20086 Mudsock Road
Wapakoneta, OH 45895
419-741-0155
www.barryfarm.com
Sorghum syrup, organic molasses, and xylitol, along with a variety of flours, cereals, and legumes. The Web site offers direct online ordering.

Madhava Honey

Lyons, CO 80504
303-823-5166
www.madhavahoney.com
Full line of fine honey and agave nectar products, available primarily at their retail location.

Wholesome Sweeteners

8016 Highway 90-A
Sugar Land, TX 77478
800-680-1896
www.wholesomesweeteners.com
Organic and Fair Trade agave nectar, honey, molasses, and sugars. The Web site includes a listing of retail stores where products are sold as well as links to outlets for direct online ordering.

Wild Organics

P.O. Box 1161
Niwot, CO 80544
www.wildorganics.net
Organic agave nectar, honey, jams, and teas. The Web site offers direct online ordering.

TEA, NONDAIRY MILK, AND OTHER BEVERAGES

Blue Diamond—Almond Breeze

P.O. Box 1768
Sacramento, CA 95812
800-987-2329
www.bluediamond.com
Almond Breeze almond milk. The Web site includes a listing of retail stores where products are sold as well as direct online ordering by the case.

Lifeway Kefir

6431 W. Oakton Street
Morton Grove, IL 60053
877-281-3874
www.lifeway.net
Kefir and lassi products. The Web site includes a listing of retail stores where products are sold as well as direct online ordering for some products.

Nancy's Yogurt

Springfield Creamery
29440 Airport Road
Eugene, OR 97402
541-689-2911
www.nancysyogurt.com
Kefir and yogurt. The Web site includes a listing of retail stores where products are sold.

Pacific Natural Foods

19480 SW 97th Avenue
Tualatin, OR 97062
503-924-4570
www.pacificfoods.com
Organic almond, rice, and hemp milks; soy milk; teas, soups, and stock. The Web site includes a listing of retail stores where products are sold as well as direct online ordering.

Scharffen Berger Chocolate Maker

601 22nd Street
San Francisco, CA 94107
866-972-6879
www.scharffenberger.com
Unsweetened natural cocoa powder, unsweetened chocolate bars. The Web site offers direct online ordering.

SpecialTeas, Inc.

500 Long Beach Boulevard
Stratford, CT 06615
888-365-6983
www.specialteas.com
Black, white, herbal, organic, matcha, decaffeinated, and green teas. The Web site offers direct online ordering.

Stash Tea Company

P.O. Box 910
Portland, OR 97207
800-826-4218
www.stashtea.com
Black, white, herbal, organic, matcha, decaffeinated, and green teas. The Web site offers direct online ordering.

Though this book was written using the most recent research available, new food sources are being established constantly. Updates can be found at www.flavorfirst.com.

ACKNOWLEDGMENTS

This book would not have been possible without the support of countless colleagues and friends who contributed valuable expertise, insights, humor, and spirit to this project.

The entire Rodale team is a joy to work with, and I'm grateful for all the behind-the-scenes work that goes into the finished product. Editor extraordinaire Julie Will provided valuable feedback, insight, and guidance as the book took shape. Rodale publicist Emily Weber gave this project crucial visibility and support. Christina Gaugler, Nancy N. Bailey, and photographer Rita Maas deserve my heartfelt thanks for transforming my plain text into such a gorgeous, enticing package.

I am indebted to my agents, Mary Lalli and Bill Stankey of Westport Entertainment, and my publicist Gary Stromberg for their support and belief in this project and all of my work.

Chef Andrew Hunter, friend and business partner, infused this book with energy and inspiration from the get-go. After ten years of remote collaboration, it was wonderful to meet finally in person, to cook and break bread together as this book took shape!

The family of registered dietitians whose work informed and inspired this book is vast. My colleagues at the American Dietetic Association, and especially the community in the Food & Culinary Professionals' group, provided invaluable guidance.

My priceless assistant, Catherine Thorpe, provided unending support, kept my Web site humming and email newsletters polished despite her continual book deadlines. My friend and fellow dietitian Cheryl Kurowski offered crucial and creative guidance to our team—I'm so glad we've reconnected after many years apart.

Many friends kept me grounded with generosity, good cheer, culinary wisdom, scientific curiosity, and spiritual guidance: Claudia Sansone and Rob Hampton, Melissa Roberson, Robin Kline, Jill Hunting, Bill Frazier, Mary Quest, Marie Feldman, Susan Bowerman, Jennifer Ford, Judi Flanagan, David Yoder, and Gordon and Suzi DuPries. Karen and Steve Price, Paula and John Beritzhoff, Patricia Treible, and Paul Skittone kept me sane throughout the process and patiently endured and tested my recipes.

Napa Valley Pilates and my personal trainer, Ines Donnelly of NapaFit, kept me active, de-stressed, and in shape while I tested and sampled these recipes over and over!

Leslie Rudd, Roger Hartley, Mark Tate, and Chris Cavazos inspired me to take nutrition beyond my small kitchen to buy a farm, where I continue to learn about growing delicious ingredients for my recipes.

The Central Market Cooking School has ardently supported my books and teaching and has hosted countless classes that give me the opportunity to meet enthusiasts of all stripes. Many of these students became Facebook and Twitter friends and newsletter subscribers, whose questions and conversation inspire me daily. I love Texas!

To everyone at NBC and Reveille—executives, producers, and crew of *The Biggest Loser*, especially Mark Koops, Todd Lubin, and Chad Bennett—thank you for all of the opportunities! *The Biggest Loser* medical expert team, Dr. Rob Huizenga, Dr. Michael Dansinger, Dr. Sean Hogan, and Sandy Krum have lent me invaluable guidance and support. Julie Ann Harris, Kat Elmore, Drew Lewandowski, Kristin Mearns, Amanda Quinn, and Kevin Goddard make my trips to the Ranch seamless and VERY fun—thank you!

Finally, I thank all of my private clients as well as the contestants on *The Biggest Loser*—past and present. I wish I could list each of you by name. You were with me in spirit as I wrote this—especially the recipes. I cannot thank you enough for letting me be a part of your transformation and life's journey. You have each inspired me personally and for that, you have inspired this book.

INDEX

Underscored page references indicate boxed text. **Boldfaced** page references indicate photographs.